DAY BY DAY

Tales and Trails of a Grandfather

Richard L. Day

Day By Day
Tales and Trails of a Grandfather
Author: Richard L. Day
Editor: Marla McKenna
Proofreader: Lyda Rose Haerle
Cover Painting: Sali Day
Interior & Cover Layout: Griffin Mill

All images are courtesy of Richard and Sali Day, unless otherwise noted.

Paperback ISBN: 978-1-957351-61-2
Hardcover ISBN: 978-1-957351-63-6

PUBLISHED BY NICO 11 PUBLISHING & DESIGN
MICHAEL NICLOY, PUBLISHER
MUKWONAGO, WISCONSIN
www.nico11publishing.com

Be well read.

Quantity order requests can be emailed to:
mike@nico11publishing.com

Printed in The United States of America

DAY BY DAY

Tales and Trails of a Grandfather

Richard L. Day

Dedication

Linnea Michele Harrington
1979 – 2021

This book is dedicated to our beloved granddaughter, Linnea Michelle Harrington (née Janowski), 1979-2021. She took her journey to heaven on June 8, 2021. Stage 4 Metastatic Breast Cancer claimed her life. She leaves behind her husband, Ryan, and their two daughters, Keagan 13, and Keely 12, and her loving family and friends.

We rejoiced at her birth and were blessed, as she grew up into a beautiful, talented young woman. She was loving, kind, and generous. Her many, many friends are a testament to her friendly and caring nature. She loved her family, especially her two daughters, Keagan and Keely. She fought so hard during the eight-year battle with cancer in order to instill good life lessons into her daughters.

We miss you Nonnie Girl. We are comforted by knowing that your soul and spirit are with God in Heaven—the beautiful Heaven you saw on four occasions while in hospice and described to your mother. We know you are in a place where there is no more death, or crying, or sorrow.

Your loving grandparents,

Gpa Dick and Gma Sali

INTRODUCTION

On a rainy day in Girdwood, Alaska, August 14, 2006, I began writing my life stories for our grandchildren: Linnea, Richard, Justin, Jordan, Brittney, and Natalie. They were all born in Alaska—except for Jordan, who was born in Wisconsin. He would have liked to have been born in Alaska, but now, he happily lives there. Also, I have included some Scriptures as they pertain to the stories.

My father, Olney Bark Day, or O.B., as everyone called him, was a closed book when it came to his childhood and growing up in Chicago. The few bits and pieces that I gleaned from family members about the Day family, revealed that my father's childhood had some tragic events. This may have been the reason my father did not care to tell us about his childhood.

I would rather let my grandchildren and our great-grandchildren, see the life I have lived with both wins and losses, as I sought the path God has chosen for me. Hopefully it will enable them to see the good choices I have made and see the resultant benefits. Also I hope they will see the results of my poor choices and learn from them to make better choices in their lives. I cannot protect them from the trials and tribulations they will have in their lives, but my stories, hopefully, will encourage them to push on, in faith, through the struggle and not give up.

Scripture tells us that we live in a morally and spiritually broken world. With that in view, it is fair to ask, "How then should we live?" I hope that our grandchildren and great-grandchildren will learn at an early age that the most significant, the most worthwhile, the most joyful life we can live, is one of gratitude, generosity, forgiveness and love, and serving God.

PART I

GROWING UP

EARLY CHILDHOOD

ROW, ROW, ROW YOUR BOAT

Everyone has to be born. For me this happened on May 6, 1933, in a cottage on Goodrich Lake near Sherwood, Michigan. At 2 a.m., my father drove to Sherwood to wake up the country doctor. Then the doctor hopped into his Model A Ford and drove out to our cottage. There was no electricity in the cottage, so a Coleman lantern had to do. It did—and I arrived.

When I was two months old, my mother Wilma and her sister Lydia, both Chicago girls, decided to go for a midnight boat ride. It was a calm, warm summer night. The full moon was casting its reflection on the still waters. Only the chirping hum of crickets and an occasional deep croak of a bullfrog could be heard. Little baby Richard was fast asleep on the screened-in porch.

Mom and Lydia hopped into the rowboat and sat side-by-side on the middle seat. Each took an oar and proceeded to leisurely row out into the lake. Neither had any experience rowing a boat, but they were in no hurry to get anywhere. All is well, life is good, just floating along beneath the stars out in the middle of the lake.

Suddenly, the stillness of the night was loudly interrupted by the screams of a baby echoing out across the lake. Little Richard had awakened and wanted immediate attention! Mom and Aunt Lydia heard my cries and quickly went into action. Each grabbed her oar and pulled with all her might. It soon became apparent that something was seriously wrong. Instead of going in a straight line for the cottage dock, they discovered they were going in a big circle. The problem was that one oar was longer than the other!

As I continued screaming, they

Author, one year old. 1934.

remembered the rattlesnakes that resided in the nearby strawberry patch. What if one had gotten inside the porch where I was in my crib? It didn't take long for the city girls to figure out how to adjust their rowing and make a beeline for the dock. The screaming baby was soon rescued, and thus ended their midnight boat ride. No rattlesnake either.

DAYS ON THE MOVE

The only jobs available around Sherwood at the time of my birth were agricultural in nature. My dad, Olney, along with my uncles, would work at odd jobs—cutting wood, cleaning stables, milking cows, and digging up potatoes for nearby farmers. Dad, whose talent was in running truck lines, was soon tired of this low-paying, back-breaking work. There were greener pastures in Chicago, my family's hometown. So, when I was about 18 months old, the Day family packed up and headed for the big city. We moved to the south side of Chicago, into one of the many red-brick apartment buildings.

TRICKY DICKEY

One of my two-year-old tricks, according to my mother, was to take a dozen eggs from the refrigerator and break them all—not on the kitchen floor, but out on the living room carpet. Also, I got this hot idea to take my new box of crayons and melt them on the radiator. Cast iron radiators preceded baseboard heaters. They were waist-high room heaters through which hot water flowed. In both cases I created a real mess for my mother to clean up. Such a sweet kid I was.

COLD FEET

The neighbors across the hall from our apartment were a railroad detective and his wife. They had no children and sort of adopted me. On Saturday mornings, everyone slept in … except for little Richard. I would get up, go across the hall, and climb into bed with the detective and his wife. My feet were cold as ice, and he loudly exclaimed to his wife, "Get this kid's cold feet away from me!" He gave me the nicknames of "Richard Alawishes" and "Dickey Day Shay with a Belly Full of Hay."

Our stay in Chicago was short, as Dad soon took a job managing Gordon's Truck Line in Memphis, Tennessee.

DICKEY'S TEA PARTY STUNT

Tea party transportation.

We lived in Memphis from the summer of 1935 to 1940—age two through six for me. Summers were very hot and muggy. On one of those hot summer days, my mother decided to have a tea party for the neighborhood women. I was playing outside in the front yard, riding my favorite tricycle. Evidently the heat overcame me, so I took off all my clothes and ran into the house—right through my mother's tea party! This obviously livened things up. The women pointed fingers and screamed with laughter! A three-year-old boy can get away with stunts like that.

MOTHER'S DRIVING DISASTER

I remember my dad buying a brand new, four-door, 1938 La Salle automobile. It was the precursor to the Cadillac. It was a long black gangster type car with big whitewall tires, chrome trim, chrome bumpers, and a chrome front grill. We would cruise along at 80 miles an hour when 50 was considered fast.

Dad hired a neighbor boy to teach my mother how to drive. At 5-foot-2, she could barely see over the hood of our LaSalle. Also, there was no power steering in those days to help a small woman turn such a heavy car. On the way home from her first lesson, Mom made a turn that was too wide and slammed into a telephone pole. The pole broke off at the base, swung way out, then right back into the front grille, smashing it! That was the end of Wilma's driving … Forever!

THE PINK PALACE

Memphis was the home of a very wealthy and creative businessman whose name was Clarence Saunders. He gained his wealth by developing the first self-service grocery stores; Piggly Wiggly. They still exist today in parts of the Midwest and the South.

In the early 1920s, Saunders built a stone mansion called The Pink Palace. It was a large, beautiful, castle-like home—with manicured lawns, beautiful gardens, and a long winding drive up to the entrance.

Inside the mansion were mounted big game animals taken on an African Safari. You can imagine how very impressive this was to a five-year-old boy. It was a great adventure for me and my little friends to take a long hike to the mansion and play on the manicured grounds. As a kid, the hike seemed like we had walked a mile or two, but having gone back as an adult, I now realize it was actually only a few blocks. It is strange how the world shrinks and time accelerates as we grow older.

The City of Memphis became the owner of the Pink Palace in 1923 when Mr. Saunders was forced to sell due to financial losses in the New York Stock Market. It is now a museum. A truth from Scripture applies: *"Man is but a puff of wind. He moves like a phantom. The riches he piles up are no more than vapor. He does not know who will enjoy them"* (Psalm 39:6—my paraphrase).

DICKEY DAY'S PYROTECHNICS

While in Memphis, at age five, I got a hold of some small firecrackers. It must have been near the Fourth of July. I proceeded to light them and throw them as far as possible. They would explode with a loud bang! Great fun! Then … I had a dud! It didn't go off! I waited … and waited … and waited for the bang, but nothing happened.

Time for action! I went over to pick up the fire cracker. Just as my hand was above it, BANG!!! It exploded! The blood poured out of the palm of my hand like a shower head. Oh, did it hurt! I can't remember what happened next, but I'm sure my dad came to the rescue and took me to a doctor. There's an old photo that shows me holding my injured, bandaged hand behind my back.

MISS HOPPER'S RECITAL

My dad enrolled my sister and me in a private grade school. It was owned and run by Miss Hopper. In addition to our academic subjects, we all were required to take tap dancing lessons. I was a first grader and my sister, Maurine, was in kindergarten. Once a week we had tap dancing lessons. We stood along the wall holding onto a bar or radiator with one hand as we practiced our steps … "Left foot, tap toe, tap heel, switch hands, right foot, tap toe, tap heel, turn, turn." … Yuk! I was a very unhappy camper on tap dancing lesson day.

Finally the day came for Miss Hopper to show off her tap dancing class to the parents. This necessitated that we have a recital! Eighty-four years have passed since that recital and I can still remember every detail in three-dimensional color. My sister was a little dancing fairy. She wore a pink net costume with wings, pink tights, and some sort of halo attached to her head piece. All the boys wore a white silk blouse with long puffy sleeves, Dutch Boy bib overalls of dark blue silk, and black, patent leather tap shoes. Beautiful, just beautiful!

Miss Hopper lined us all up behind the stage curtain, the music started, and the curtain rose … the performance was on! Maurine danced around on her tiptoes in her fairy costume with the rest of the little fairies, while the boys did our routine. Tap, tap, turn; tap, tap, tap; arms up, arms down, turn around; tap, tap, yuk, yuk, yuk; *God, please get me out of here!* The parents oohed … ahhed … cried … took pictures … clapped … and laughed at our goofs. I turned three shades of red and hated every moment. It was the closest I ever came to a mental meltdown! That was the end of my stage career, with no possibility of going on to the bright lights and the fame of Broadway. Good riddance and no regrets!

MICHIGAN VISITS

GRANDMA RILEY'S FARM

One of the few constants in my childhood was my Grandmother Riley's farm. During the Depression of the late 1920's, my Grandmother Riley's family and my Great-Grandmother Van Dam's family lived in South Chicago. The men in the family worked for the Illinois Central Railroad or the Pullman Car Company.

The economic crisis of that time caused many men to lose their jobs. This evidently prompted my great-grandmother, Wilhelmina Van Dam, and my grandmother, Jennie (Van Dam) Riley, to seek a solution to surviving these hard times. In the Chicago newspaper they found a 19-acre fruit farm for sale near Colon, Michigan, and must have decided that this was the way to survive the Depression. Grandma Riley bought the farm and gave her mother, my great-grandmother an acre. They then moved their families to Michigan.

My family, and the families of my mom's sisters—Lydia, Helen, and Madge, gathered at Grandma Riley's farm for vacations and special holidays—especially the Fourth of July, Thanksgiving, and Christmas. The families traveled from Memphis, Chicago, and Ft. Wayne, Indiana, to Grandmother's house. This was between 1935 and 1945.

FIRECRACKER SCARE

One summer we were vacationing at Grandma Riley's farm for the Fourth of July. My sister Maurine was five-and-a-half years old. Someone gave me some firecrackers. I had totally forgotten my previous experience of blowing up my hand. My next "bright idea" was to have my sister look into the end of an eight-foot water pipe—while I set off a small firecracker at the other end. I reasoned that she could watch the explosion.

Well, without realizing it, I had just turned the water pipe into a gun barrel. When the firecracker exploded, it propelled sand in the pipe, right into Maurine's eye. Maurine and I were both screaming.

Dad came to the rescue and took Maurine to the doctor in Colon. I hid in the tool shed, still crying … terrified my sister would be blind in one eye and it was all my fault. I remember Maurine returning from the doctor having this big bandage over her eye. Thankfully, she had no permanent eye damage.

LIFE ON THE FARM

Maurine, Teddy, Dick; 1940.
Dad's LaSalle in the background.

The farm paralleled the St. Joseph River just east of the little town of Colon, Michigan. It was primarily pear, apple, peach, and cherry trees. Gram always planted a large vegetable garden as well. Teddy, Gram's white Spitz dog was her only pet. There were a few white Leghorn hens and one large, nasty rooster who tolerated only Gram entering the chicken coop. For everyone else, his kingdom was off limits—and you could expect him to attack you at any moment.

The big event of family gatherings in the summer was the evening meal in the front yard, with a huge bonfire. Most of the time, my dad and my uncle, Johnny Gales, caught a bucket full of rock bass and bluegills from the St. Joe River to fry. Gram's garden provided tomatoes, corn on the cob, wilted lettuce salad, and green beans. Add to that, potato salad, lemonade, ice tea, and marshmallows to roast on a stick. Makes me hungry just thinking about it.

I remember one time, when we were all sitting around the fire after dinner. Great-Uncles Henry and Johnny Van Dam were playing their accordion and guitar for all of us to sing along … when suddenly a mole popped up out of the ground and ran around and around the fire. This, of course, startled everyone. The men laughed, and the women screamed! It was a great time to be a kid. There was always something exciting happening on Gram's farm.

UNCLE JOE'S SURPRISE

One night, Johnny Gales and I went down to the river to go fishing. Teddy followed us along the dark trail. We built a big fire for warmth as well as to chase away the mosquitoes. My Uncle Joe, Johnny's older brother, found out where we had gone. He decided to sneak up on us and scare us.

The trail to the river went through the old orchard, into the woods, and down a steep hill. There were long heavy vines hanging from the trees. As Joe was sneaking up on us, he could see the reflection of the fire light in Teddy's eyes. A bright idea popped into his head. He ran as fast as he could down the trail, leaped up, grabbed one of the vines and yelled, "It's a lion. It's a lion!" as he swung over the top of us, way out over the dark river. Suddenly, the vine broke. Uncle Joe fell into the river fully dressed. Did we ever laugh. Teddy barked and barked. It was another great night of fishing on the ole' St Joe!

MY GREAT IDEA

In the farm house, Johnny Gales and I slept upstairs in what had been the attic. Houses in those days were rarely insulated. It was freezing in the winter and hot in the summer. When the orchard was in full bloom, the fragrance of the blossoms filled our bedroom. At night, we could look out the screened window and see the sky filled with stars, like sparkling diamonds. The brilliant moonlight would also shine into our bedroom. The summer night air was filled with the music of thousands of chirping crickets to lull us to sleep.

Gram had recently added a flat-roofed living room and bedroom attached to the original steep-roofed house. At that time, there was no bathroom in the house, only an outdoor toilet at the edge of the old orchard. Probably about midnight, I needed to go to the bathroom really badly—too much Kool-Aid, lemonade, or iced tea. Going to the outdoor biffy alone in the dark was not appealing to a six-year-old boy. Scary things like spiders, snakes, and wasps, hung around outdoor toilets. So, the sensible solution to me was to aim through the screened window. That was a great idea, I thought, as I quickly crawled back into the warm, cozy bed. All was well; I had fooled those spiders, snakes, and wasps!

The next morning, Johnny and I joyfully went down stairs to have breakfast. Gram, we noticed, was madder than a wet hen! She marched us to the living room and pointed to the ceiling. There, as plain as could be, was a large circular stain. Gram demanded, "Who did that?" Johnny looked at me ... I looked at Johnny ... he laughed, and I trembled. How did I know the new roof leaked? Well, I figured Gram needed to know this before a big rain came. So ... actually, I did her a favor, don't you think?

WEEKENDS AT THE FARM

COLON-BOUND

Just before the beginning of the Second World War, 1939-40, we moved from Memphis back to Chicago. On Fridays, after work, Dad piled us in the car and we headed for Gram's farm in Colon, a three-hour drive away. When we crossed the Indiana-Michigan state line, Dad rolled down the car window and cheered, "Yay! We're in Mitchigan—where the air is cleaner, the water is better, and the fishing is greater!"... plus whatever else he could make up about the greatness of Michigan. He'd say some lines from an old song—"Oh, how I wish-i-gan ... I was in Mich-i-gan ... down on the farm."

Dad's enthusiasm has affected my loyalty to Michigan all my life. That includes attending The University of Michigan and being a lifelong fan of the Michigan Wolverines football team. Yes, we still like to shout—"GO BLUE!!"

There was no electricity at the farm. That came with Rural Electrification in the early 1940's. Gram had kerosene lamps, used fuel oil to cook with, and had a large pot bellied wood stove with which to heat the house. Sometimes we used candles or a Coleman lantern for light as well.

We arrived at the farm long after dark. Gram would greet us and then give me a flashlight and tell me what canned vegetables and fruits to get out of the cellar. She always let me select one favorite thing that I wanted, knowing that it was always a jar of cherries. Then, Teddy and I headed for the back of the house. There, I would lift the cellar door and shine the flashlight down the narrow, stone stairway into a small dirt-floored cellar—dusty and spider-webby, scary and spooky. I was glad Teddy was with me. Down the stairs we went. I shone my flashlight around on all the wooden shelves which were stocked full with canned jars of green beans, yellow beans, corn, tomatoes, carrots, pickles, peas, peaches, pears, and always my favorite, cherries! I grabbed whatever Gram wanted, and last, of course, my jar of cherries. Then, Teddy and I climbed the stairs, closed the cellar door, and quickly headed back to the front door. I can still see this scene so clearly … even these many years later.

ROOSTER ATTACK

One of my daily chores on the farm was to gather eggs. This was an okay thing, but not my favorite job. The problem was Gram's nasty Leghorn Rooster objected to my presence in the chicken yard. That was "His territory" and "His kingdom"! Gram usually had him fenced off when I went into the coop to collect the eggs. The hens didn't mind being disturbed by my gathering the eggs. They ran around and clucked a lot, but did not peck at me.

One day, I went into the chicken yard and did not check to see where Mr. Rooster was. While I was in the hen house gathering eggs, he decided to ambush me. All of a sudden, there he was—flapping his wings, cackling, jumping up, and trying to stick his spurs into my legs. Fortunately, I had some leather high top boots on and he only spurred me once. Gram heard me yelling and came running full speed with a broom in her hand. She whacked that rooster a couple times, chasing him off. She saved my bacon that day. The rooster didn't learn a thing though. He always challenged anyone who went into the chicken yard except Gram. That was "His" domain, and he was determined to stay in command … and that, he pretty much did!

ST. JOE RIVER THERAPY

The St. Joe, or Saint Joseph River, was a significant focal point of life on the farm. On hot summer days, the whole family went down to the river by a path that led down a steep hill from Great-grandmother Van Dam's nearby house. The party included Gram, Great Gram, Great-grandfather Lucas, my parents, and all of my aunts, uncles, us kids, and

St. Joseph River.

the dog. The meandering and slow-flowing river was mostly shallow, clear, and the bottom was sandy. We used it for fishing, swimming, bathing, and for cooling ourselves.

I can remember seeing my Great-grandmother, Wilhelmina Van Dam, in an old cotton print dress, wading out into the middle of the river with her walking stick. She would plant the stick deep into the sandy bottom and sit, with only her head above water, while holding onto her walking stick. We had no air-conditioning, but the river worked well. We all loved the Ole' St. Joe.

GRANDMA RILEY'S MIRACLE

Great-grandmother Van Dam and Grandmother Riley, were both committed Christians. Grandmother Riley, through all her trials and tribulations, always remained strong in her faith. When any of the family stayed at Gram's, she always took her grandchildren to Sunday school and church. At Gram's house we always prayed before our meals. My favorite Grandma Riley's faith-building story is about an unusual loaf of bread.

In the hot summers, Gram did her washing out in the yard. This was before she had electricity. She had a wooden rack that held two large galvanized wash tubs: one with hot soapy water, and one with cold water for rinsing. There was a hand-cranked wringer between the tubs to squeeze the soapy water out of the clothes as they went from one tub to the other. Sometimes my job was to turn the crank on the wringer.

One summer day, Gram was doing her wash and lamenting her difficult economic circumstances. She didn't even have money for a loaf of bread. Being a woman of faith, she began to earnestly pray and ask God to supply her need—in this case, a loaf of bread. Before the wash was done, a man pulled into the driveway in a big car. He jumped out, introduced himself, and informed Gram that he was starting a "Bakery Route" to offer fresh baked goods to the farmers in the area. He told Gram that he hoped she would become one of his customers. Then he presented her with a loaf of bread saying, "Here's a free sample of what I will be selling."

I love this story. It blesses me every time I tell it. It's a good example of Matthew 7:7—"Ask and it shall be given you; seek, and you shall find; knock, and the door shall be opened to you." Also, "I have not seen the righteous forsaken, nor his descendants begging for bread" (Psalm 37:25). This is a Hallelujah story.

GRAM VAN VISITS

MY DUTCH HERITAGE

My great-grandparents, Lucas and Wilhelmina Van Dam lived on an acre next to Grandma Riley's farm. Great-grandma Van was very short and round. She had a gentle nature and was always busy at some task around the house. I remember one of Great-Gram's expressions was, "You dasn't do that!" instead of, "You must not do that!" Also, she described things being "Too dear" meaning "Too expensive." Great Gramma Van's rule for the outdoor toilet was: "Use only two sections of tissue." There was always a Sears and Roebuck catalogue on the seat for backup. This was a very frugal household.

Great-Grampa Van was tall and thin—taller than six feet. He had a red mustache, was a man of few words, and except for Sundays, always wore bib overalls. I can't remember any discussions I ever had with him. He always had a large vegetable garden that supplied lettuce, carrots, tomatoes, radishes, and other fresh produce for the table.

OBEDIENT LITTLE BOY

I would visit them on my way down to the river to go swimming. Great-gram had a small cook house, separate from the main house. The front half had a wood-fired cooking stove, small refrigerator, and a table and chairs. The back half had a step-down part with a concrete floor and drain where Great Gram did her laundry. She always wore her wooden shoes, her "Klompen", because of the wet floor. This must have been part of her Dutch tradition. Great Gram was always kind to me and granted me "first great-grandchild" privileges. She made a wicked "head cheese," which is a type of gelatinous lunchmeat. When I visited her, I dutifully ate the sandwich she made for me. However, I never really learned to like head cheese sandwiches.

HIDDEN TREASURES

One afternoon, I followed Great-grandma Van down into her mysterious dirt floored basement. Narrow pathways led us to years of saved treasures. I saw a set of ceramic toy molds that my father used to pour hot lead into to make toy soldiers. I wish I had asked Gram if I could have them. There were canning jars, old clothes, tools, a few books, and other odds and ends—nothing of heirloom value. Also, I spotted a jar with the label—"Pieces of string too short to use". I can hear you laughing!

Lead toys from my dad's toy store, dating back to 1930.

BEEHIVE JIVE

Their oldest son, my Great-Uncle Johnny, was a hunchback. I had always assumed he had cotracted rickets as a child. In conversation with my second cousin, Verna Hall, Johnny's niece, I learned the real cause.

When Johnny was a young boy, he and his friends were jumping off a barn roof into a large bank of fluffy snow. By the time Johnny jumped in, the snow was hard-packed and the force of his impact caused his spine to collapse. The end result was his hunchback condition. He was fortunate to miraculously survive such an injury. This stunted his growth and his height was less than five feet.

Great Uncle Johnny went on to become a barber in Colon. I used to get my 65-cent haircuts from him. He always used a small stool to stand on when he cut hair.

Uncle Johnny also raised honey bees as a hobby. When it came time to harvest the honey, he cut the wax sides of the honeycombs off, then placed them in a basket in a large barrel. On occasion, it was my job to turn the crank handle on the side of the barrel that caused the basket to spin. The centrifugal force caused the honey to flow out of the honeycomb and into the barrel. Then Johnny poured it into jars and sold his fresh honey to local farmers.

I remember one time we were out in the orchard watching Great-uncle Johnny gather honeycombs from his beehives. He put dried sumac buds into a hand-held bellows and lit the sumac. This produced a biting smoke that could be directed at the bees. When the bees slowed down, he could lift the honeycomb frames out of the hive. Johnny wore a straw hat with netting attached, long sleeves with rubber bands around his wrists, and gloves for protection. Well, that wasn't always enough.

We were watching from a safe distance, when all of a sudden Johnny began to leap and cry out: "Hot ziggety, hot ziggety!" Uncle Johnny, who never swore, had been stung really good and so it was "Hot ziggety! Hot ziggety!" as he hopped around the orchard. A bee had gotten up his pant leg. Ouch! Oooo, Ouch!!

GOSPEL DUO

My other Great Uncle, Uncle Johnny's younger brother, Henry, had contracted polio as a young child and one of his legs was severely affected. This caused him to walk with an obvious limp.

Both Henry and Johnny played piano, accordion, guitar, and sang in beautiful harmony together. They were a unique duo when they went out to nearby small churches to preach the gospel and sing. They were always well-received.

SUNDAY RULES

Great-grandmother Van Dam always observed the Scriptural admonition of keeping the Sabbath Day holy. I'm sure this stemmed from her Dutch Reformed faith traditions. She did not cook on Sunday, so all her food was prepared on Saturday. Sunday was to be a day of rest, and on that day no work was to be done, which included cooking. She always warmed up her precooked food for Sunday dinner. The Van Dam Sunday included Bible reading and hymn singing. There was no card playing, no loud "worldly" music, and no horseshoe playing. Reading the "Comics" in the Sunday paper was marginal. Sometimes Henry played the piano, and we sang hymns.

JOHNNY GALES

MY BOYHOOD HERO

I suppose we all have our "childhood favorites." My uncle, Johnny Gales, was mine. He was my mother's younger brother, and Gram Riley's youngest son. He was 13 years older than I and in his late teens. He had a great mop of curly brown hair and often went around barefoot. In summer he stayed out late with his friends then slept out in what we called the "screen house." His lifestyle always put a strain between him and Gram, who had high hopes for her youngest son. Johnny could play a mean harmonica, had a beautiful singing voice, loved a good story, loved to laugh, and also liked a good prank.

PRAYER PRANK

My uncle, Joe, Johnny's older brother, the most serious and spiritual man in the family, was often asked to pray at mealtime. It was his habit to, as we say, "Pray around the world." In other words, pray lengthy prayers. One holiday, when we had a big family celebration at the farm, Johnny knew that Joe would be asked to pray. Everyone gathered at the table and sat with bowed heads in dutiful silence as Uncle Joe began his prayer. Everything went well for a couple minutes. Suddenly, the prayer was interrupted by a loud, blaring, trumpet! As this surprise interruption continued, everyone tried to keep their reverent composure. Soon, however, snickers turned into laughter, and Uncle Joe's prayer was drowned out! Johnny Gales, holding his sides and laughing uproariously, had deliberately engineered this whole prank by starting Gram's record player before he came to the table. Uncle Joe was a good sport about it though … "Will someone pass the green beans, please?"

FISHING BUDDIES

My most favorite pastime was fishing, and we did a lot of that! Usually, Johnny Gales and I went out into the woods along the river, and there, in the wet black soil, we dug for red worms. We got a hundred or so and put them in soup cans filled with dirt. Then, we gathered our cane poles, fish stringer, tackle box, and headed for the river. If my dad was there, he always went with us. The wooden river boat we used was a narrow 16-footer with a small 9hp outboard motor. We knew where several deep holes were downstream.

*O.B. Day on the
St. Joe River*

They were filled with logs and stumps, but that's where the fish were. We placed our bobbers on the line to the correct depth, added split-shot sinkers as needed, put a couple wriggling red worms on our hooks, then tossed the bait out into the hole. Usually we had an immediate bite, and pulled in a rock bass, bluegill, or sunfish. Sometimes the fish was strong enough to pull your line into a snag—like a limb or a stump. If that happened, it was "goodbye fish," "goodbye hook," and maybe, "goodbye line and sinker too!" We caught lots of fish and we lost lots of hooks and sinkers. Yes, it truly was a child's paradise, and I enjoyed every day at Gram's farm on the Ole' St. Joe.

When we lived on Palmer Lake in Colon, Johnny and I would fish for Crappies and Pike. We needed minnows for that type of fishing. Johnny knew where the best places were to net or trap minnows. In addition to fishing with them we sold them to the local bait shop and made a few extra bucks.

On hot rainy summer nights, he taught me how to take a flashlight and grab night crawlers that were stretched out on lawns or the sidewalk. These also were sold to the bait dealer for five cents each. Picking up nickels was a high paying job for a kid. "There's a nickel, there's another nickel, and another!" A kid could make a fortune just pulling up wet, slimy, wiggly night crawlers.

FRIDAY NIGHT DRAMA

On many Friday nights in the summer when I was seven years old, Johnny and I walked the mile and a half from Gramma Riley's farm into Colon. He would hang out with his friends while I went to a movie. I had my 25-cent allowance, which was a real chunk of change. It gave me 10 cents to pay for a movie ticket, 5 cents for popcorn, and 10 cents for a "Looney Tunes" comic book or candy.

After the movie, Johnny and I walked back to the farm. If Johnny wasn't ready to go home, I would walk back to the farm alone. When I reached the last street light on the edge of town, I still had about half a mile of narrow gravel road to walk to reach the farm. That was always a very scary half-mile. If a car came along, I jumped off to the side and hid in the tall weeds until it passed. I didn't want to ride with strangers.

On moonlit nights, the trees and bushes cast their shadows across the road. Rabbits, attracted by the heat of the road, scurried off into the weeds as I came along. My effort to sing a bit didn't seem to help.

There were spooky things out there in the dark that made weird sounds, and try as I might, I could never see them, but I just knew they were there! It was the longest, loneliest, and scariest half-mile I ever walked.

When the distant lights of Gram's farm came into view, my heart leaped for joy, and I could breathe easy again. Teddy would hear my coming, and dash out—barking and wagging his tail to greet me. We ran to the farm house as fast as my little legs would carry me. "Safe at last." "Safe at last!"

RETURN TO COLON

WARTIME IN COLON

In the fall of 1940, during World War II, we moved from Chicago to a home on Palmer Lake in Colon, Michigan, with a population of 1000. I was in the second grade. Franklin D. Roosevelt was president.

The bombing of Pearl Harbor by the Japanese on December 7th 1941, brought America into the war, which was now against both Japan and Germany.

Shortly thereafter, my Uncle Johnny, like thousands of young American men, joined the military to serve our country. Johnny really looked sharp in his Navy "Blues" and I was so proud that my uncle was in the United States Navy! He served on a minesweeping ship in the Caribbean and then in the South Pacific. I was so sad to lose my best friend and fishing buddy.

Most young men 18 to 25 joined, or were drafted, into the Army, Navy, or Marines. Their families would hang a banner with a blue star on it in their front window representing a son or daughter in the military. Some windows had more than one blue star on the banner. Some had a gold star representing "killed in action." All of America was sacrificing for the war effort.

The war caused significant changes in the lives of American families. There were shortages of gasoline, tires, and certain foods. Most American families had to deal with these wartime shortages.

I remember my mom having me jump on my bike and go to the

A&P grocery store early in the morning so I could get to the head of the line. This gave me first dibs on buying butter, sugar, coffee, bananas, and Hershey's chocolate, which were all in short supply. Farmers, and people with "war sensitive" jobs, had a higher priority for gasoline than the average citizen.

My father was employed by the Army Base, Fort Custer, in Battle Creek. His job as Traffic Manager, was considered to be War Sensitive, so he was given a "B" fuel stamp, which allowed him to purchase the gasoline he needed to travel the 65-miles round trip to work every day.

We had "blackout" drills where all the lights in the town had to be turned off. Then, police would drive around and check to see that all occupied buildings were dark. Schools sold War Bonds, and everyone saved aluminum foil and grease. Many others collected milkweed pods to be stuffed into life preservers for flotation.

In August of 1945, the war ended. There were great celebrations … with the biggest bonfire I had ever seen! Soon, "Johnny came marching home again," a line from a popular wartime song. Time for Johnny and me to catch up on our fishing … and we did!

CHICKEN IN THE ROAD

The last memorable episode with Johnny was the time he decided to buy a Harley Davidson motorcycle. I was 14 at the time in the summer of 1947. Johnny located the motorcycle for sale in the nearby town of Coldwater. We hitched a ride for the 17 miles to purchase and pick up the bike.

This was my first motorcycle ride. Johnny did a couple trips around the block to practice before I climbed on to sit behind him for the ride home. It was great excitement to hear the roar of the Harley motor and feel the wind as we sped back to Colon.

The route home wound through the southern Michigan countryside. As I looked ahead over Johnny's shoulder, I could see a big, white, dead chicken lying in the road. We were traveling about 45 or 50 miles per hour. I quickly reasoned that if I could kick that chicken the feathers would fly up like a great cloud of snowflakes. What great fun! What a great sight! What a great idea! I told Johnny to steer close to the chicken so that I could kick it and watch the feathers fly.

A 14-year-old does not know the laws of physics in situations like this. Briefly, when an object traveling at 45 miles per hour, like my shoe attached to my foot, strikes a stationary object, like this dead, four- or five-pound chicken, a tremendous force is necessary to bring the stationary object up to the speed of the moving object—my foot! I dropped my foot down to road level to kick the chicken right through the goal post. Wham! The pain was excruciating. I thought I had broken my ankle and dislocated my right hip. I looked back, the chicken was still in the road and not one feather was in the air. I don't think it moved an inch. Johnny laughed and I cried.

PALMER LAKE PARADISE

Summers during my grade school years were spent swimming, boating, and fishing. In winter, we ice skated, went sledding, played hockey, and fished through the ice. Dad made an ice fishing shanty. It was a 6x6x6-foot windowless tar paper shack. It had a 2x4-foot hole in the bottom and a small fuel oil heater in one corner. We cut a hole in the ice to match the hole in the bottom of the shanty, then slide it over the hole. Many hours were spent sitting in this warm shack fishing for bluegills, perch, and sunfish. It was exciting to watch them swim into our view.

To make the fish more visible, we dropped yellow corn kernels into the water. They sank to the dark muddy lake bottom and reflected light. Everyone always had a spear just in case a big pike came along. A couple of times, on school days, I suddenly contracted a very bad cold and had to spend the day recuperating while fishing in Dad's fish house … cough, cough, cough! I loved those days.

RADIO ADVENTURES

After school, I hurried home and made myself a peanut butter, banana, and honey sandwich. Then I would lie down right next to a small AM radio and listen to my favorite serial stories. They were sponsored by breakfast cereal companies like Kellogg, General Mills, and Ovaltine. Each lasted 15 minutes. Their names were: *Little Orphan Annie, Tom Mix, Jack Armstrong—the All-American Boy, Sky King, The Lone Ranger,* and *Sergeant Preston of the Yukon, with his dog King.* The stories were full of adventure with good guys versus bad guys. The good guys always triumphed over the law breakers. The sponsors would always offer something for a certain number of cereal box tops and a quarter. I remember one offer was a decoding ring. I had to have it because a coded secret message was given out at the end of the program and I needed to decode the message. Hey … this was War time! Serious spy stuff! I loved my programs, I didn't ever want to miss a single one.

FOURTH FUN

Fourth of July celebrations were always big during the war. The Colon High School Marching Band led the nighttime parade. Every homemade float, farm tractor, horse, civic organization, pet, and kid were welcome to make up the parade. Mom and Dad dressed my sister Maurine up as Miss America, and me as Uncle Sam. We entered the "Best Costume" contest and won first place!

Then, I entered a pie eating contest. All the pies were placed on a waist-high table, our hands were tied behind our back, and then the starter signaled "Go!" We stuck our face into the pie and ate as fast as we could. I won my age group of 10-year-olds. I had blueberry pie from ear to ear. Next, I entered a contest where they placed a dime in the bottom of a pie plate and filled it with flour. Again, our hands were to be kept behind our back. We leaned over the flour-filled pie plate and blew out the flour in order to find the dime. By the time we were done we looked like a ghost with two dark eyes! I can't remember who won that contest. I did get the dime though.

TWO AGAINST ONE

In my third-grade class were twins, Alan and Arlon King. We were friends. One school day in winter, we had a heavy, wet, snowfall. During recess, we all started throwing snowballs. This evolved into a snowball fight between me and the King twins. Snowballs were flying back and forth. I got the winning edge with a few direct hits … but somehow, I was the one turned into Mrs. Frye, our teacher. I was accused of starting the snowball fight. I pleadingly explained to her that it was two against one. This fact didn't matter a whit to her when it came time for the punishment to be meted out. I had to stay after school and write 300 times on the blackboard, "I will not throw snowballs; I will not throw snowballs; I will not throw snowballs." It's important to remember … life isn't always fair. "In this life you will have tribulation" (John 16:33).

LITTLE THIEF

In the fourth grade during lunch hour, we would sometimes run to the nearby downtown area, which consisted of one block of stores. This was, of course, if we had a nickel or dime to spend. Brast's Variety Store was a favorite place to go because of their selection of comic books, toys, and candy. Being wartime, there was also a big selection of military items.

On this particular lunch-time trip, as I wandered through the store I spotted a display of sterling silver rings. They had insignias or crests of the different military branches; Army, Navy, Marines, and Air Force. I think they cost about 35 cents, which was much more than I had. My little fourth grade heart lusted strongly for one of those rings. Some power unknown to me, just guided my little fingers right to one of those rings. I quickly put it into my pocket and headed out the door. My heart was racing as fast as my legs, as I headed back to school.

All afternoon I kept that ring in my pocket, never took it out, and never wore it. Just like Bilbo Baggins and his *Ring of Power*. The guilt I felt from stealing it grew by the hour. It was like an elephant on my back. Sleep that night was difficult because of the thought of what I had done, and I still had the ring hidden away. I knew that I didn't dare tell my parents!

The next day I couldn't wait for lunch hour to come. The ring was burning a hole in my pocket and in my conscience. I watched the school room clock as the minutes dragged by. As soon as the lunch hour bell rang, I headed to Brast's store. When no one was looking I put the ring back in the display and ran out of the store, so thankful to be rid of my guilt. That was the beginning and end of my being a thief!

TUNE IN TUNE OUT

In the fifth grade, we were encouraged to join the band. Mr. Flowers was head of the music department and was also the band director. He would meet with us and our parents and help us select an instrument. I think the band needed clarinet players, so Mr. Flowers nudged me in that direction. I didn't think the clarinet was a very masculine instrument, but I took lessons from Mr. Flowers and faithfully practiced a half-hour every day. I went into a small bedroom, set up my music stand, and produced lots of squeaking and squawking at first. We were seated in the band according to ability, with the first chair in the first row being the "honored" seat. This seat was occupied by Nadine Michael. Well, of course, the whole first row, four seats, were occupied by girls … "teacher's pets." No, they probably just practiced more than the boys. I think I worked up to the second chair in the second row, but the clarinet wasn't for me. I wanted to play football—not a clarinet!

"HEY, DICK … LET'S — ?"

One warm spring day, my friend Louie Weinberg came by my Grandma Riley's house to walk to school with me. He had lived on a farm on the outskirts of town, but when his father died, the family moved into town. Louie was the sixteenth of 16 Weinberg children. Louie was a sixth grader and I was in the fifth grade.

I can hear him saying, "Hey, Dick, let's skip school today!" This sounded good to me, although I'd never done such a disobedient thing. Louie was bolder than I and more of a risk taker. I didn't recognize that temptation might come from the voice of a friend.

Gram had gone to work at the Lamb Knit sweater factory, so there was no one to catch us. The school was a couple hundred yards away and two houses shielded us from view. We heard the tardy bell ring and figured we were safe to begin a day of fun, freedom, and goofing off, doing whatever we pleased. It was a warm sunny day, so we decided to hide under a spruce tree out in Gram's front yard. We told stories, we laughed, we chewed on grass stems, we caught crickets and grasshoppers, and we wondered what was going on in school.

After a few hours, we decided to sneak down the hill to Swan Creek. This was a small stream that flowed down from the Palmer Lake Dam and then right behind Gram's house. We sat by the creek, talked, threw rocks into the water, caught a few crayfish, and watched for fish to swim by. Every hour we could hear the large clock tower bell at the school ring … and every hour we got more and more bored.

By noon we discovered that we were victims of our own scheme— prisoners in Gram's yard! Gram's house was off limits while she was at work. The school was only a short distance away, so we couldn't go that direction. The other direction was towards Louie's house, and we couldn't go that way. Besides, two grade school boys wandering around a small town during school hours was very suspicious. Ugh! Trapped.

We spent a very long, boring afternoon; going from the spruce tree … down to the creek—from the creek … back up to the spruce tree. We squashed a few ant hills and tried to catch a frog or two. We lay on our backs and looked at cloud formations. The hours slowly dragged by and were peeled out by the school clock bell tower. Finally … finally … three o'clock came and we knew school was out. We had pulled off our little trick and had been tricked in the process, which of course, we did not admit.

Louie went home, and I decided that I wanted my baseball glove. It was in the closet of my classroom. I waited until I knew the school was emptied out, except for the old school janitor, Joe Stoll. I stealthily crept into the school and up to my classroom. Sure enough, my ball glove was in the closet, and I retrieved it safely. Just as I was leaving the room, who should happen upon the scene … but Mrs. Flowers, my fifth-grade teacher. I quickly developed and demonstrated a bad cold and cough, which of course was the reason for my not being in school that day—a really lame excuse. Mrs. Flowers looked at me very suspiciously, but the ruse worked. Louie and I never mentioned skipping school again and never did we repeat our little fiasco. "Foolishness is bound up in the heart of a child; the rod of correction will drive it far from him" (Proverbs 22:15).

WATER BOY

One day I was over at Louie's house, and his older sisters were preparing dinner. The water bucket was empty—so Louie's older brothers, Leslie, nicknamed "Wink," and Lauren, elected Louie and me to get the water. The Weinberg's were not on city water, so their water was pumped by hand from a well out in the yard. There was a narrow concrete walk from the pump to the house. To liven things up in the "Weinberg way," they made us fill the bucket right up to the rim. I did the pumping and then Louie had to carry the full bucket to the house without spilling a drop. For every drop they counted on the concrete sidewalk, we each got a slug in the shoulder administered by Wink and Lauren. Not just a tap, but a hard punch. My shoulder was black and blue for several days. Hey, life was tough at the Weinberg's; survival of the fittest!

LEAD ON, LOUIE

One hot summer afternoon, Louie stopped by to see if I wanted to take a hike down to the Swan Creek railroad bridge. I was all in for the adventure. Louie never wore shoes in the summer, and the soles of his feet were like shoe leather. I always wore shoes and never thought of this difference—or, as it turned out, of his advantage. I decided to join him in going barefoot. So … off we went, at first on the sidewalk, and then along the paved road. Things were going great!

We had gone about a half mile, when Louie wanted to take a short cut across the school athletic field. This meant we had to walk through some tall weeds to get to the mowed ball field. Louie just took off and so I followed. Within two steps, I'm oohing, and ouching, whining, and crying! We were walking right through a patch of sand burrs and they were sticking into my tender feet. I stopped, and yelled to Louie, "I can't go this way!" He yells back, "Oh, come on, you big sissy!" Louie was never very patient or compassionate. I gingerly picked the sand burrs out of my feet and back-tracked in order to take a different way. Louie went on ahead.

I caught up by the time Louie reached the railroad tracks. We had come almost a half mile so far, but now had another quarter mile to go down the tracks to our destination—the railroad bridge over Swan Creek. On hot days like this, when the temperature was close to 90° F, we could look down the tracks and see the heat radiating off the steel rails and rail bed, in wave-like shimmers. Of course, Louie just proceeded to casually walk on one rail like a circus tightrope walker. I had a dilemma ... I couldn't walk between the rails because the rail bed was made up of sharp cinders and they often covered the ties. This prevented me from hopping from tie to tie. I put my bare foot on the rail to follow Louie and it was like standing on a burning hot frying pan. I yelled to Louie, "Hey, I can't make it, can't go any further." He turned around, and with a frustrated look, came back to me and said, "Ok ... get on, I'll carry you." So, down the track we went with me riding on Louie's back. Louie walked the burning rail and never fell off—and never missed a step. Louie was bigger than I was, and as strong as an ox, so I wasn't much of a burden.

We got to the Swan Creek railroad bridge, watched the fish swimming, climbed down to the creek, and just messed around like boys do. After a while ... we had had our fill of Swan Creek—so it was back up to the tracks. Louie said, "Climb on," and off we went down the tracks to the road home.

Louie was a rough and tumble guy, but a good friend. He could have been a college football star as a running back—if a coach had taken him under his wing academically and athletically. He died at a young age, and I feel cheated that life did not allow us to spend more time together. I am brought to tears when I recall such good and precious childhood adventures with my friend—Louie. I miss you Louie. I hope to see you again—in Heaven!

THE MUFFIN MAN

Probably the most painful day in grades 4 through 7 was what I will call "Music Day." As part of our music education, Mr. Flowers, the Band Leader, would come to our classroom every week with his little pitch pipe, and the painful exercise would begin. He had us stand in a circle around the room—boy, girl, boy, girl. Then we sang a wretched little song called, "Oh, Do You Know the Muffin Man?" To this day I have no idea how it got into our music education curriculum. The lyrics are simple and stupid, at least for a sixth-grade boy. It's a call-and-response song. Mr. Flowers stood in the middle of the circle and chose one student to start the song. We did this acapella, so he gave the pitch, and then the person selected danced around and stopped in front of a classmate of the opposite sex and sing, "Oh ... do you know the muffin man, the muffin man, the muffin man, Oh ... do you know the muffin man who lives on Drury Lane?" Then the person sung to had to respond, "Oh ... yes I know the muffin man, the muffin man, the muffin man, Oh ... yes I know the muffin man who lives in Drury Lane." Then the couple joined hands and skipped around the room as everyone sang the muffin man chorus. The skipping couple stopped in front of someone and sang the chorus and then they would reply, join hands with the first couple, and dance around the circle as all sang. This process repeated itself until all had been chosen, and the dancing troupe got larger and larger. As you might surmise, classmate romances were part of the process and brought giggles and finger pointing. This might seem like fun to an observer, but to most sixth and seventh grade boys it was an extremely uncomfortable experience. You can bet Louie and I wished we had skipped school on one of those days. Give me my

C- in Music and let me out of here! No wonder I've never been fond of muffins.

A BOY'S SALVATION

The summer of 1944, the year before the war ended, I was 11 years old. My family was still living on Palmer Lake in Colon. Gramma Riley found out that the Potawatomi Indians in the area were having a camp meeting on a farm near Athens, Michigan. Gram decided to go to the camp meeting and invited me to come along.

The three-day meeting was held in a beautiful wooded grove. A large meeting tent was erected and families set up their personal tents nearby. I had my own small tent. Meals were served in a dining tent. I guess there were at least 200 people at the meeting. The weather for this outdoor event was perfect; hot and sunny every day. The Potawatomi chief and other Indian families were there. No particular church denomination was the sponsor, just Christians gathering from the South Central Michigan area.

Every day there was an afternoon service and an evening service. There was lots of singing, testimonies, and vigorous preaching! Each day, a different evangelist would preach the Gospel at both services. It was a very cordial and joyful crowd of Michiganders. I can't remember every detail of that time, but every day there were a couple softball games played and horseshoe matches. The Potawatomi Chief brought along his beautiful feathered headgear and wore it for those who wanted to take photos with him.

One afternoon, there was a horrible motorcycle accident on the nearby highway. I remember running, along with many others, down to the highway to witness the tragic scene. Several motorcycle riders were badly hurt, bleeding, and crying out in pain. A wrecked car, and damaged and broken motorcycles were scattered on the highway. The camp meeting people quickly began to attend to the injured riders until an ambulance and police arrived. The whole scene sickened me, so I ran back to my tent and hid from all the commotion and trauma.

That evening, Gram and I went to the service. The initial atmosphere was somewhat somber due to the accident, but everyone heartily entered into the singing and prayers for the injured motorcycle riders. The preaching was, as usual, enthusiastic … and, as usual, long. I sat obediently by my grandmother's side. At the end of each service there was always an altar call. The preacher explained how our human nature is sinful, and that our sins offend God and separate us from Him. Our need was to be forgiven of our sins, to be reconciled to God, and receive the promise of Eternal Life. "For by grace you have been saved through faith, and that not of yourselves; it is a gift of God" (Ephesians 2:8).

As the altar call proceeded, people went down to the front, kneel to be prayed for, and confess their sins. They then expressed their faith in Jesus as their savior. I remember Gram saying to me, "Dick, don't you want to go forward and ask Jesus to come into your heart and be your Savior?" As an 11-year-old I had no deep knowledge of sin, justification, or sanctification, and had not pondered the meaning of eternal life. I did have an inherent conscience that was very sensitive to knowing and doing what was right versus what was wrong. Obeying my parents, my grandmother, my teachers, was just what I did, with little complaint. Of course, I trusted that my grandmother always knew what was best for me, so I went forward and knelt at the bench along the front row. The preacher came along and laid his hands on my head and prayed for me. I repeated words of repentance for my sins and accepted Jesus as my Savior. There were no miraculous signs, no thunder and lightning, no fireworks, but as I look back over the past 79 years since my salvation, I know God has had His hand on me. Thanks, honor, and praise are due Him.

SPINSTER STRICT

The grades in Colon schools were combined, so the sixth and seventh grades were in the same room. Our teacher was Miss Alice Grimes. She was a spinster and had been a governess for an English family in London. Just as WWII began, she moved to Colon to care for her aged aunt. She had an English accent, sharp features, and dark red hair which was pulled back into a bun. She dressed well in mostly rich colors, and she always wore black shoes with two inch heels. She was our hardest and most strict teacher. I remember her writing a math problem on the blackboard. Then, she strolled up and down the aisle, asking me, or others, to solve the problem. She would stand beside our desk and urge us on, saying, "Come on Love, come on Love, what's the answer, what's the answer?"… all the while rapping us on the back of our hand with her wooden ruler; rap, rap, rap … rap! It didn't hurt, but it was distracting. Fortunately, I was good at math.

"HERE … MISS GRIMES"

When I was in the sixth grade, Harry Blackstone Jr. was in the seventh grade. Harry's father was "Blackstone," the world-famous magician. Harry was a tall, good looking, and intelligent boy. He was also a pest in the classroom.

One spring day, Harry was acting up in class. Miss Grimes had had enough of Harry and called him up to her desk. On the desk was a vase full of pussy willow branches loaded with fuzzy buds. Miss Grimes had Harry bend over and then she took a handful of willow branches and proceeded to swat Harry on the derrière. It didn't hurt Harry a bit, as he was wearing heavy corduroy pants. Every time she gave Harry a swat, a few buds flew off and fell to the floor. Harry, remaining bent over, picked them up and reached up and put them on Miss Grime's desk, saying, "Here Miss Grimes, you can have these back." "Here Miss Grimes, you can have these back!" This infuriated Miss Grimes … but it was extremely humorous to all of us watching. Finally, in disgust, she sent Harry back to his seat.

Looking back, we all loved and admired Miss Grimes. She was strict; she was heavy on discipline, but she had a good heart. She cared for her students and wanted them to succeed in life. God bless you, Miss Grimes … you were the best!

COUNTY FAIR

Every September, the St. Joe County Fair was held in Centerville. This was always a big event for me. There were craft exhibits, produce displays, all sorts of new farm equipment, new cars, and all kinds of farm animals that "4H" kids brought. The Colon High School Band marched and played in competition with all the other county schools. There also was horse racing, fireworks, and a big stage show at night. And, of course … cotton candy, taffy, food, food, food, and lots of fun rides.

I took in every event possible. My dad gave me five dollars, which was a small fortune to me. I would pay 25 cents and get on a wild ride, get sick, and throw up until the ride stopped; then go have something to eat and get back on another ride with the same results. I just loved going to the fair.

One time I went to a booth that had a bunch of men shooting .22 caliber rifles. I could barely see over the counter. The object was to try to shoot at a row of wooden matches all lined up about 10 feet away and light a match. Three shots cost a quarter. If you lit a match, you won a dollar! I watched those big guys shoot and miss or at best break off the matches. After a while I got up enough courage and gave the booth attendant my quarter. With much fear and trembling, I stood as tall as I could, rested the rifle on the counter, took careful aim, then slowly squeezed the trigger, and POW! A match lit! There was total silence at the booth. All these big guys looked down at me. Finally, the guy next to me says: "This is the kid to take squirrel hunting." Everyone laughed. I don't think I fired my other two shots, just took my dollar and ran off; more rides, more throwing up. That was a great day for a twelve-year-old kid.

If I try to pick a time in my life of 90 years that was the happiest, it has to be my grade school years in Colon, especially the fourth and fifth grades. Life consisted of fishing, swimming, boating, sledding, ice skating, fun at school, riding my bike, the county fair, selling strawberries that Mom and Dad had picked, and trapping muskrats—

just the happy life that a ten- or eleven-year-old kid should have, with no adult responsibilities. I have wondered why adult life can't be that way. It must have something to do with Democrat or Republican policies, i.e. … "Politics" and the "IRS!"

MOVING AGAIN

HOOSIER TIME

It is now 1947 and my family has moved from Colon to Marion, Indiana. I should mention that my father, Olney Bark Day, or "O. B. Day," had a special talent in the trucking business. He had the ability to take a broken-down truck line and turn it around into a profitable business. This usually took about three years. Seldom did he profit much; it was always the owners who did. Dad's talents were always in demand, and with it came the frequent moving of our family. We had moved 11 times by the time I graduated from high school.

FLYING FLOP

In the seventh grade I began to play sports and build model airplanes. I worked for hours and hours on balsa wood stick model planes. The glue and paints we used at that time had lethal ingredients about which we were ignorant. The chemical vapors destroyed brain cells. I've always wondered how many IQ points I lost building those model airplanes.

My biggest project was fabricating a "P-38 Lightning," which was a WWII fighter plane. It had twin rubber band-powered engines and a 36-inch wing span. I painted it to look authentic. For the first flight, I wound up the rubber band engines and then climbed up on a tall fence post. I reasoned that when I released the propellers the plane would climb, fly over to a nearby field, and glide to a nice landing. I got all set, held the plane up as high as I could, released the propellers, and gave the plane a hard toss. It started off okay, but after about a ten-foot flight it banked sharply to the left and headed straight for the ground! Crash! Crumple! Crunch! My beautiful P-38 Fighter plane—all in pieces! Hours and hours of work destroyed in less than a minute. I could have cried, and I did. Oh well, as they say, "It's the journey ... not the destination that counts." I never had the heart to put that plane back together again.

FROM C to C to C

All students at Marion's McCullough Jr. High had to take art and music. Additionally the boys had to take woodshop and the girls, home economics. The music department staged an operetta every year; some Cowboy Western thing, and everyone had to sing a short solo part as a requirement to get a grade in music. At age 14, my high tenor voice was changing. If I started my part in a low key, so as to be able to make the high notes, I had no volume. If I started in my normal tenor voice, I couldn't hit the high notes without my voice cracking. Add my stage fright to this quandary and we had one very unhappy camper. Memories of Mrs. Hopper's tap-dancing recital came flooding back. I somehow suffered through an embarrassing performance ... and got my C in music.

Our art teacher was Mrs. Cooper. I go from Hopper to Cooper. She was, let's say, less than pleasant ... actually a grouch! She didn't like my effort to draw and color a vase of irises. Although I didn't know it at the time, I was, and am, and always will be "red-green" color blind. Can't help it, it's genetic—so another C- in art. I probably burned my report card that year.

The only other thing I can remember about the seventh grade is that our woodshop teacher took special delight in the fact that Dick Day and Donald Knight were in the same class. He seated us next to each other so that when he called the roll, he could say: "Day ... Knight" and then laugh along with the rest of the class. Ha! Ha! Ha! Very funny ...very funny!

Our woodworking project was to make a tie rack for our fathers. I worked very hard on this project, but got only a C grade for my effort.

I was very disappointed to give my dad a poorly graded tie rack. He deserved better. As an adult, I love to build things, but woodshop was not my favorite class, and not my favorite teacher. The Scripture previously quoted seems to bear repeating: "In this life, you will have tribulation."

PAPERBOY

While I was busy making C's in art, music, and woodshop, building model airplanes, and spending hours shooting baskets with friends, I also found time to start my first entrepreneurial adventure, namely a paper route. Marion, a town then of about 20,000 people, had its own local paper. It was published on Sunday through Friday.

A neighbor and classmate, Verne, had a paper route of about 100 customers. He had had it for at least a year and was growing tired of the restrictions it placed on him. He asked me if I would like to take over his paper route.

He arranged for us to meet with the paperboy supervisor so that he could interview me for the job. All went well, and I was approved to take over the route. I followed Vern around on his route to learn the streets and homes of the customers. On Saturdays there was no paper to deliver, so on that day he had me follow along as he collected the weekly charge of 25 cents. All of this was done on our bikes. The whole route was about three or four miles from paper pick-up to finish.

Verne handed his large canvas carrier bag to me, and said "Good luck!" I was in business, a small cog in the American free market system. My routine was to leave our house around 4 p.m. and ride my bike a couple miles to the pick-up point. There, I would join five or six other paper boys. We waited for a truck to drop off our large bundles of papers. Then we all folded our papers into a 6 inch x 6 inch square and loaded them into our bags. The folded shape enabled us to throw the papers long distances onto the customers' porches. Well, most of the time it hit the porch. There were no roadside mail boxes to put the paper in.

I took my heavy bag filled with a hundred folded papers and fastened it to my bike's handlebars and rode a half-mile to the start of my route. At first I wasn't really accurate with my paper throws. If I missed the porch. I had to dismount my bike, retrieve the paper, toss it again to the porch, get back on my bike and head for the next customer. This, start ... stop ... start again, extended my time to complete my route to at least three hours. By the time I had delivered the papers for a few weeks I had the time down to about two hours.

As a 14-year-old, I did not do a business analysis, which would have revealed my hourly wage was pathetic, nor consider that I had committed to a seven day a week responsibility. Rain, shine, wind, snow, ice, mean dogs, no matter, I had to deliver the paper to my waiting customers. The Sunday paper was always heavy and couldn't be folded to throw. A couple times on Sunday in rain storms or heavy snow, my father had me put the papers in the back seat of the car. He slowly followed me around my route as I delivered the papers door to door. "Thanks, Dad!" Well, I was young, strong, and free from any self-criticism of the value of my time. I wanted to please my parents by doing a good job and being successful at my first job.

When Saturday came around, I dutifully hopped on my bike around noon and headed for the first home on my route. Most people were home on Saturdays and had a quarter to hand me. Some customers left an envelope with a quarter in it taped to the screen door. Some paid me monthly. I'd get an occasional tip of a nickel or a dime. One customer gave me a weekly quarter tip if I would ride up his long driveway and put the paper inside the screen door.

Most of my customers were middle class families, but I did have a few very poor families. I remember one time I tapped on the door of one of my poor customers. A young mother with a small child in her arms answered. I said I was there to collect for the paper. She had a small change purse and slowly picked out a dime, two nickels, and five pennies and handed them to me. I felt like I should have returned them to her. In 1947 a loaf of bread cost 13 cents, a dozen eggs about 50 cents, and a gallon of gas 15 cents. So, at that time, even a quarter was of significant value to some families. Yes, I had a few customers who always tried to avoid paying me. My recourse was to just stop delivering their paper. They whined and complained, and tried to come up with some sort of sob story, as they begrudgingly paid me the money they owed. Most of my customers were "salt of the earth" and a pleasure to deal with, but in this life, there's always a few rotten eggs.

My monthly income from my labors was $20.00 plus, maybe $6.00 or $7.00 in tips. I kept the paper route from August until April. We were going to move back to Michigan when school was out. My great reward was a shiny, new, beautiful Schwinn bicycle, to replace my beater of a bike. I tried to save every dollar I made until I had $75.00 to purchase the bike. It had a leather seat, and a cream and blue paint job, with red pinstriping. The wheel rims were chrome and it had a spring loaded front wheel suspension system. All my friends had to take it for a ride. Oddly, I have no idea what happened to that bicycle.

A FISHING SURPRISE

We moved back to Colon for my eighth-grade year. Dad finished his work in Marion and then was hired to bail out another truck line in Cape Girardeau, Missouri. My mother, Wilma, my sister, Maurine, brothers, Jim and Robert, and I squeezed into Gramma Riley's tiny house in Colon.

A favorite place of mine to fish was at the Palmer Lake Dam spillway which was only a couple blocks away. The dam held back the waters of Palmer Lake, and was the beginning of Swan Creek that flowed behind Gram's house. The dam was originally made of logs and later reinforced with concrete. The lake water flowed over the top of the dam, dropped about six feet to a horizontal spillway, then flowed about 12 feet and dropped a couple more feet into a pool below the dam. The water churned, and bubbled, and foamed, as it poured into the pool. Through the bubbles and foam, you could see pointed log ends projecting out from the base of the original dam into the spillway pool. This all made for good fishing. There was a small island out near the center of the pool.

One fine summer day, I was standing out on the spillway fishing with my dad's fly rod. I had a pair of old leather work boots on. I was casting my bait out into the pool trying to catch a big rock bass. After about a half hour of no luck, to my left, I caught sight of a piece of rope which had come over the dam, then a bucket tumbled by, and then, a few moments later, a little boy came over the dam. The water carried him quickly across the spillway and down into the bubbling pool below the dam. I had no time to think about what to do. I tossed my fly rod off to the side and dove in after the boy. I couldn't see anything because of the bubbles and foam, but immediately two little arms were tight around my neck. How did this little kid find me so quickly? It was all I could do to get my head above water in order to get a badly needed breath of air. My leather boots were now like lead boots on my feet. I swam with all my strength for the island. The kid had a death grip on me and now was perched up on my shoulder. Finally, I could just touch the bottom with my toes. This enabled me to sort of bounce along toward the island shore and into shallower water. With great effort I managed to get this five-year-old into my arms and carry him through shallower water to the pond bank. There, I put him down, and without a word, he scooted off for home.

Later that evening, Mrs. Oldenberg, a friend of Gramma Riley's, came to the house and profusely thanked me for saving her little son, Alan. The owner of our Shell gas station was a friend of the Oldenburg's, and when he heard the story, he rewarded me with an old gaff-rigged sailboat. Several years later, a friend of mine from Memphis, Seth Giem, helped me fix it up and take it to Austin Lake near Kalamazoo, where Seth spent the summers.

After many years, my wife Sali and I were in Colon for Grandmother Riley's funeral. Mrs. Oldenberg was there and introduced me to a very tall young man in his 30's. She said, "I want you to meet my son, Alan. He is the little boy who went over the dam." I got a big hug from them both. It was both a sad day and a happy day, a day for mourning and a day for rejoicing, and plenty of tears. Gramma, a faithful servant of God, was now with Jesus, her beloved Savior.

HIGH SCHOOL YEARS
BACK IN DIXIE

It's now September 1948 and time for the Day family to move again! Off we went to Cape Girardeau, Missouri, where Dad was resurrecting another truck line, Kimball Trucking. I started the ninth grade and played high school football. Our time in Cape Girardeau, however, lasted only a few months.

We then moved to Memphis. The wealthy Gordon family, owners of Gordon's Transport, had coaxed Dad back to Memphis a second time, to take their dead truck line and breathe some life into it. My mom was a saint. Every time Dad said, "Min, (her nickname), we are moving," she just quietly began packing. This wasn't just once or twice, but at least 14 times that I could count. The pictures were barely hung on the walls when it was time to take them down again.

It was the usual financial story; Dad made big bucks for the truck line owners but was rewarded very little for his dedicated, hard work. Things were always done on a "hand shake" basis—no written contracts. He was impatient for results in business, yet he would sit in a boat and patiently wait for hours for a fish to bite.

TREADWELL HIGH

My 9th and 10th grades were spent at Treadwell High in Memphis, Tennessee. This is where I met Seth Giem in a ninth grade Civics class. We discovered that we both spent the summers in nearby towns in Michigan. Seth's father was raised on a farm between Vicksburg and Kalamazoo. During our ninth-grade summer, Seth and I hauled my sailboat over to his farm, part of which bordered Austin Lake. It was an old boat, a bit rotten, and awkward to handle, but we had fun fixing it up and learning how to sail it.

At Treadwell High, I played football and basketball. Also, I should mention that in the South, boys were required to take R.O.T.C. (Reserve Officer Training Corps) all four years of high school. We were required to wear our Army uniform one day a week, take military classes taught by regular Army sergeants, and drill with our M1 Garand rifles.

I continued to build model airplanes when I had time. I built the planes, then my buddy, Dudley Gaouette, put his engine on them. Dudley flew the plane, and if he had a crash, then I made the necessary repairs. He then refastened the engine, and off we'd go again. Great fun! I have breathed in so many airplane glue fumes that I'm lucky to have any brain cells left.

About this time, at age 15, I remember taking a Sears and Roebuck catalogue, a 3x5 card, and making a list of all the things I needed to go on a big game hunt in Alaska. I can only guess that the origin of this idea went way back to the fourth grade when I listened to the 15-minute radio serial stories of the adventures of *Sergeant Preston of Yukon!* The radio announcer said, in a fervent voice: "Sergeant Preston of the Yukon … and his dog, King." It must have made a strong impression on my young mind—as I eventually moved to Alaska.

A HARD-EARNED "A"

I went back to Colon to live with Gramma Riley for the first semester of my junior year. The second semester I attended Central High in Memphis. My courses were Physics, American History, English, and Geometry. Geometry I understood and loved; it was like eating candy for me. The first test given by the teacher, Miss Mauzy, had 10 questions. I had a white plastic protractor which gave me a surface to write on with a pencil and then erase my work with a swipe of my finger. The protractor was an L shape with the longer leg on the bottom and a 180-degree arch on top of the bottom leg. I did my entire test work in pencil on the back of the protractor.

A few days later the exams were graded and the grades announced. When the class was seated, Miss Mauzy stood before us and made a little speech. It seemed that someone in the class had gotten a score of 100 on the test; however, this person did not turn in their work papers to show how they obtained the answers. There was a long pause … and then she looked at me and said "Richard Day, please stand up before the class," I stood at attention in my R.O.T.C. uniform! Then she proceeded to question me in front of the class as though we were in a courtroom and I was on trial. How did I get my answers? Where were my work papers? What did I use to write on when I worked out the problems? I was totally embarrassed—blushing red in the face and neck. I could feel the beads of perspiration on my forehead. I wanted to bolt and run from the classroom! My ROTC uniform jacket pocket fortunately contained my trusty protractor and I fumbled around and produced it. I handed it to her and said that all my work was done on the back of the protractor. She carefully examined the protractor, slowly turning it over and over in her hand. "Ah Ha!" she said, "Yes, yes, I see, I see some smudgy figures are still here. Well, Richard, since you didn't turn in your work papers, I can't give you a 100 even though you answered all the problems correctly. Your grade will be recorded as 99. You may sit down Richard." After the class had left, she pulled me aside and asked me if I had plans to go on to college. I said I had none. She encouraged me to try for a scholarship and definitely go to college. Another spinster like Miss Grimes, somewhat stern, rather strict, but loved her students and wanted them to succeed in life. God bless you, Miss Mauzy … but you really put me through the ringer.

SEWANEE MILITARY ACADEMY

My friend from Treadwell High in Memphis, "Bubba Davis," his nickname for "Wooldridge Wells Davis," was attending Sewanee Military Academy. SMA was 50 miles west of Chattanooga, Tennessee, in a beautiful mountain setting. It was a prep school associated with Sewanee, The University of the South, and had grades 8 through 12. I was struggling with going to high school in Memphis, and my dad asked me if I wanted to go to SMA with Bubba. As I look back on that day, I can see the hand of God was at work in my life when I truly needed it!

Sewanee Cadet with
Aunt Madge.

The Headmaster, Colonel Fasick, came to our house in Memphis to interview my parents and me. In the process, he gave me a $200 football scholarship. This helped with the $1500 tuition, which would be about $14,220.00 in today's dollars.

Sewanee was patterned after West Point Military Academy. We had to wear uniforms, take military classes, drill with our M1 Garand rifles, eat, sleep, and study according to a rigid schedule. Our instructors were mostly retired WWII Army officers. Some were West Point graduates. All were men.

Every Sunday, our battalion of 300 cadets marched about a mile to a beautiful Episcopal chapel on the university campus. We were in full parade dress. The officers had colorful waist sashes and swords. Everything was spit and polish. A Color Guard led, followed by the band, which was followed by three companies of the cadet corps. On warm, sunny, spring Sundays, people from nearby towns came to watch the colorful parade.

Most of the cadets were from wealthy Southern families. Seventy-four of the 75 members of my class went on to college. One of my classmates got the highest grade in the United States on the Naval R.O.T.C. (Reserve Officer Training Corps) examination. The class valedictorian gave his entire graduation address in Latin. I think the only person who understood the address was Professor McCrady. He was a nuclear scientist and Vice Chancellor of The University of the South.

BEDTIME MISCHIEF

The lifestyle we had at the academy was on the strict side, but boys will be boys! There was plenty of fun and pranks to be dreamed up and carried out. We lived in a four-story limestone barracks building named Quintard Hall. It was named after Charles Todd Quintard, who was a chaplain and surgeon in the Confederate Army during the Civil War.

We were required to study in our rooms from 7 p.m. till 9:30 p.m. and then had 30 minutes to get ready for bed. At precisely 10 p.m. the bugle sounded taps. As the last note played and echoed off into the night, all would be silent in Quintard Hall. We were supposed to be in our rooms and in our beds. Every day a cadet officer was assigned to be O.C. or Officer in Charge. They had to make sure that every cadet was where he was supposed to be—in his room, and in his bed, by the end of taps. The O.C. and his staff checked each floor to see that everyone was accounted for.

Well, you certainly couldn't expect 300 boys, 8th through 12th grade, to turn the lights out and obediently climb into bed at the commanded moment, now, would you? Time for some fun! The assigned pranksters positioned a waste basket on the edge of the top of the stairs on the fourth floor. Just as Taps ended and all was silent, the wastebasket was nudged by Cadet X, so that it loudly tumbled, bounced, and banged its way down the stairs. This drew an immediate response from the O.C. and he flew up the stairs yelling "Who did that, who did that? Someone's in big trouble! Someone better speak up and right now!" Total silence; no response; Cadet X was in bed fast asleep; along with all the other angelic cadets. The O. C. then started his investigation. He walked up and down the hall with his assistant, making threats, opening room doors, shining their flashlights into cadet rooms, seeking the guilty culprit. They threatened to report the whole floor if someone didn't confess. They knocked on our doors and made lots of noise and more threats. We all remained silent and unconfessing, burying our face into our pillows to muffle the laughter. I loved every second of it. Things finally calmed down. The O.C. left, uttering threats of, "If I ever catch who did this there will be hell to pay!"

The worst trick was to light an M-80 firecracker and drop it into the toilet bowl. The force of the explosion was enough to lift the toilet bowl off the floor and flood the bathroom. This was not an acceptable prank and was never repeated.

SUNRISE SERENADE

Reveille was held every morning at 6:30. We had to form up in our platoons in front of the barracks for a head count. When all the cadets in each platoon were accounted for by their platoon leaders, the Battalion

Commander would loudly give the command: "Battalion!" then the company commanders followed with "Company!" after which the platoon commanders said, "Platoon!" Then the Battalion Commander gave the command "Ten-Hut!" And then the entire battalion came smartly to attention! Following this, each company commander would report his company, "All present and accounted for!" This procedure was repeated every day. Then it was off to the mess hall for breakfast.

One cold winter morning, we were all standing and shivering in formation. Just as the Battalion Commander was calling us to attention, from a fourth-floor window blares out a voice singing, "I'm gonna rock'em, roll'em all night long, I'm a 60-minute man!" The Battalion Commander, Dan Banks, turned and looked up to the window and yelled, "Whose window is that?" Someone yelled out, "Lagomarsino's!" We all broke into laughter. Everyone knew Cadet Lagomarsino would be marching around the barracks next Saturday afternoon. We all thought the prank was worth the price. It broke the routine and brought warmth and joy to the whole Cadet Corps on a cold morning. "Young people are prone to foolishness and fads. The cure comes through tough-minded discipline" (Proverbs 22:15 MSG).

DORPH'S TRICK

The inventiveness of a bored SMA Cadet's mind was especially displayed by Henry P. Allendorph, nicknamed Dorph, when he originated the following prank. Hank noticed that there was a space between the bottom of the window screen and the window sill. This made it possible to raise the window and push out the bottom of the screen just enough to allow a pair of shoes to pass through while holding on to the laces. Then the screen is pulled back into place, and the shoes are pulled back onto the window ledge by the laces. Finally, we take a knife and tuck the laces under the bottom of the screen. Voila! The trap has been set.

Cadet Henry Bass' shoes were chosen for the prank. Cadet Allendorph took Bass' shoes and placed them outside the screen of their fourth-floor room. All was ready. The rest of us just hung around the room until Bass came in. It didn't take him long to notice his missing shoes. Once Henry spotted his shoes, he raised the window and pushed out on the screen. Goodbye shoes! Down they fell, four floors to the ground. We were all laughing, but he was ticked and had to go down four flights of stairs and outside to retrieve his shoes.

It was important to always pick someone of lower rank and smaller than us when considering this prank. Also, to pick a pair of recently shined shoes ... and a rainy day!

YANKEE DOODLE DANDY

The Cadet Corps at SMA was composed of 292 boys from Southern states and eight of us "Yankees" from Northern states. In good humor we were teased about our northern accents and occasionally had an extended verbal skirmish about the Civil War.

Because SMA was an Episcopal school, we had a chapel service every class day. We went to our first morning class at 8 a.m. and then attended chapel at 9 a.m. in our study hall. The study hall had rows of individual wooden desks. They were the typical school desk of that time with cast iron legs, a wooden seat, and wooden top with an ink well. Also in the study hall was an old upright piano. When the bell rang, signaling the end of our 8 a.m. class, all the cadets headed for the study hall. Cadet Judge, a Texas boy, could play the piano, and he always took off running—seated himself at the piano, and started pounding out *Dixie*! This song dated back to the Civil War and was a very popular tune in the South.

While my Southern classmates were standing at attention for the playing of Dixie, I would take a seat in one of the desks, which was screwed to the floor, lay my head on the desktop, and grab hold of the wrought iron legs. This didn't suit the standing Southern-born cadets. They surrounded me, pulled my hands loose from the desk legs, and forced me to stand at attention until the song was finished. It was always a great struggle to resist their attempts! Great fun, I loved every moment! I even enjoyed singing Dixie when I was alone and out of earshot; "I wish I was in Dixie … "Hooray … Hooray. In Dixie land I'll take my stand, to live and die in Dixie … "

BEAUTIFUL ALGEBRAIC TEARS

One of my most unusual days at Sewanee was in Colonel Heyward Roberts' college algebra class. He was a rather gruff, and very "matter-of-fact" guy. Colonel Roberts had been an Army officer in WWII. It was not unusual for him to smoke during class and utter an occasional swear word. We were working out some algebraic problems on the blackboard when Colonel Roberts said he was tired of Algebra and asked us if there was something else we wanted to do. We bounced some ideas around and agreed on playing blackboard chess. This went on for a while, and then Colonel Roberts sent a classmate up to the library to get a certain poetry book. When he returned with the book, Colonel Roberts opened it and began reading, in a thick Cockney accent, *Gunga Din*. The poem was written in 1890 by Rudyard Kipling. It describes the life of an Indian bhisti, a barracks boy, who faithfully served, till his death in combat with the men in a British Regiment. We sat in rapt attention as Colonel Roberts read the poem. As he neared the end, tears began to course down his cheeks. He finished the poem, put the book down on the desk, and walked out of the classroom. We all sat in silence for a few minutes, and then, one by one, got up and quietly left the room. I've never forgotten that day and have always wondered what lay behind such a touching scene.

GOD'S BALL GAME

As springtime of 1952 rolled around, the topic of where each senior was going to college became a daily event. I hadn't given it any thought. There were no college graduates in my family, so the subject was never discussed. Also, as well as not having any plans for college, there were no funds for me to attend any college.

SMA had two appointments to West Point and two to the Naval

Academy at Annapolis. I saw a note on the bulletin board regarding signing up to be examined for these appointments. A physical exam for the Naval Academy was to be held at a doctor's office in the small town of Sewanee. I made an appointment and appeared at the proper time, confident that this was going to be a snap. All was going well until the doctor pulled out a 20-page eye chart. Each page had a large circle that was filled with small, various-colored circles. Within the circles was a number, which I was to call out. I was required to get 17 out of 20 correct. The doctor slowly turned the pages and I gave him a number. This test was a total "color blind" disaster! I'd say "33." and the doctor corrected me. "No, the number is 88." I'd say "11." and the doctor said, "No, the number is 77." On a few pages, I couldn't even see a number. All of this disqualifying nonsense dated back to the early days of naval sailing ships when there were no electronic communications. In the late 1700s, the U.S. Navy began to use flags and semaphores of various colors to signal other ships. The effects of this tradition, some 250 years later, had found its way into a doctor's office in Sewanee, Tennessee … and wiped out my potential appointment to Annapolis! I could read only seven out of the 20 numbers. Thus, my "red-green" color blindness tanked my appointment to Annapolis.

"Not to worry," as the Jamaicans say. Though disappointed, I was not defeated. The West Point exam was to be held at Fort McPherson in Atlanta, Georgia. I discovered that a classmate and former roommate, Brian Head, was going to take the exam. His father, T. Grady Head, was a Justice on the Supreme Court of Georgia, and their home was in Atlanta. We arranged for a ride to Atlanta. I can't remember who did this favor for us, but I do remember staying at Brian's home.

On a sunny, but frosty March morning, Judge Head drove us to Fort McPherson. There were at least a hundred cadets from various military academies all gathered at the fort gymnasium. On the first day we took exams in math, English, history, and science. The second day was all athletic events: pushups, sit-ups, 100-yard dash, standing and running broad jumps, distance running events, and a basketball toss in the gym.

I was quarterback on the football team and a pitcher on the baseball team at Sewanee. I had also played basketball and football in most of my high school grades. During my senior year at Sewanee, I threw the discus and javelin on the track team. I remember starting to throw a football in the 7th grade. I tell you all this just to make the point that my throwing arm was in good shape. So, we did the sit-ups, the pushups, and the running. All is well, and I was happy with my performance. Now it was time to go into the gym and toss the basketball. I was looking forward to this event, but didn't know the requirements.

The gym was like a lot of small school gyms. It had a basketball court, bleachers along the sides, and a stage at the end of the court. Our group of about 20 was led down to the end of the basketball court. There we received instructions from a muscle-bound master sergeant who was in charge of the basketball toss. He told us that we were to kneel under the basket at a point behind the out of bounds line. We were allowed three throws. Two noncoms stationed about three quarters down the court marked and measured each of our throws. The longest throw would be scored and become part of our total score.

One by one the cadets took their turn to toss the basketball, while the rest of us stood by and watched. Most of the tosses were half to three quarters down the length of the court. Finally, it was my turn. I took off my jacket and tie and knelt under the basket. The sergeant handed me the basketball. I made sure I was behind the boundary line, placed the ball in my palm, slowly brought it back, like I would throw a football, and with about 75% effort heaved the ball down the court. It arched high over the length of the court, across the depth of the stage, and slammed into the back wall. The sergeant looked at me and said, "You didn't do that … I don't believe what I just saw!" The measuring noncoms lifted up their hands in a gesture of, "What do we do?" There were two colonels standing nearby having a friendly chat and paying no attention to me. The sergeant joined them and out of my hearing, discussed my throw with them.

I knelt there waiting for their decision. Eventually they came over to me and the sergeant said I could make my second toss. He handed me the basketball, but this time I had one colonel on my left and the sergeant and the other colonel on my right, observing my every move. I repeated my throw with the same technique as the first throw, but this time I put 100% effort into it. The ball, again arched high over the court length, across 30 feet of stage depth, and slammed into the back wall, even higher than the first throw. My three judges stood there in silence, looking at me, then at the distant stage wall. They soon walked off to have a private conversation. When they returned the sergeant said, "Okay, son, we don't know how you are doing what you're doing, but we think you are cheating. We can't measure your toss, so you have one last chance to give us something to measure, or else you will be disqualified!"

By now I was ticked off and didn't appreciate being falsely accused of cheating. I thought, *Take that back wall down, and I'll show you just how far I can throw this thing.* Well, I was a lowly cadet, with no recourse against the powers over me. I backed up a couple feet behind the line and disgustedly tossed the basketball out about 15 feet, got up, grabbed my tie and jacket, and walked away.

At the end of the day our total scores were posted. We needed 415 points to qualify for an appointment to West Point. I looked at the list, ran my finger down to my name, and there was my score; Richard L Day: 400 points. My heart sank and I was crushed to come so close to achieving my goal, but in the end, no prize, no college education scholarship! My classmate, Brian Head, did get an appointment and went on to graduate from West Point.

Reflecting back over the 70 years since the basketball throw, and doing a little research, there is a Proverb that describes my situation. "Whoever is patient has great understanding, but one who is quick-tempered displays folly" (Proverbs 14:29 NIV). With more patience, I should have just gathered myself and thrown the ball down the court to a lengthy, but measurable distance—hopefully, one that gained me a West Point scholarship. It would have been a great reward, and given me a college education. Very nice, but … and that's a BIG But! … I wouldn't have been drafted into the Army, gone to Alaska, become a student at Michigan, met my future wife, Sali, had our two daughters,

Holly and Heather, become an Orthodontist, and on, and on. Life has very strange twists and turns, and we never know the path God will lead us down. "In their hearts humans plan their course, but the Lord establishes their steps" (Proverbs 16:9 NIV).

The next day, lacking bus fare, I hitchhiked up to Chattanooga and on to Sewanee. It was a long day; standing along the highway with my thumb out, but it gave me ample time to think about my color blindness disqualifying me from an Annapolis appointment. And now, a "15-point" short basketball toss disqualified me from a West Point appointment. Yes, I shed a few tears, but no one was around to see them. *Move on, Richard, move on!* I needed the Scriptural words of Paul's letter to the Ephesians from the Message translation (Eph 6:10-14, my paraphrase) — "Richard, in the battles of life, you are up against far more than you can handle by yourself. Take all the help you can get, every weapon God has issued, His Word, faith, abundant

prayer, and use these to your advantage, so that when the battle is over, you are still standing!" Amen!

I loved Sewanee. I still love Sewanee. I liked the discipline, the organization, and the neatness of academy life. All my worldly possessions were contained in one upright metal cabinet at the end of my bed. The Spartan lifestyle suited me to a "T."

Sadly, the academy no longer exists; a victim of public dissent over the Vietnam War. The University, however, with its beautiful limestone buildings and scenic mountain top location, is still there. Our barracks are now a dormitory for Episcopal seminary students.

PART II

MAKING MY
OWN WAY

NAVY PIER

After graduation from Sewanee, in May of 1952, the Day family moved to Chicago. Actually, it was Oak Lawn, where my dad became the terminal manager of Roadway Express trucking company. This is the only truck line still in existence some 70 years later. Look for the big "ROADWAY" trucks on the highway. You will still see them!

I had no plans to go to college, in fact, no one in our family had gone to college, in fact, my parents had not set aside any funds to pay for a college education for me. During my senior year at Sewanee, I had overheard many conversations amongst my classmates about where they planned to go to college. I must have subconsciously absorbed this. Now that I had a high school diploma, it was time for me to decide what I was going to do with the rest of my life. As I look back to that time I know God was helping me make that decision. Somehow I found out that entrance exams were being held at the University of Illinois-Chicago, which was on Navy Pier near Chicago's downtown. I asked my father if I could take the exams, he said "yes." I passed with flying colors and enrolled in the Fall semester in Civil Engineering. My parents were more than happy to let me live at home and pay for my tuition. The drive from our home, near Midway Airport, to Navy Pier was at least 25 miles, so Dad bought me a 1948 Dodge four-door to make the long drive every day to class. This Scripture fits my circumstance. "Now unto Him who is able to do far more abundantly above all that we ask or think, according to the power (Holy Spirit) that works in us" (Ephesians 3:20).

The highlight of my entry exam was that I scored in the top 2 percent of entering freshmen in math. I loved math and was proud that I had done so well! However, I then proceeded to flunk my Trigonometry course! Our rather rigid, stuffy professor gave us 10-problem tests, and expected us to complete the test in one hour. I, nor most of the class, could never complete all 10 problems in one hour. I would get six correct and four with no answers. That was a grade of 60, no matter how you looked at it! The highest final grade earned in the class was a C+. I repeated the course a couple years later at Michigan, and got my "A"! Go Blue!

I took a Reserve Officer Training Corps (ROTC) course, and we did our drill practice out on the end of the pier. Often the waves of Lake Michigan splashed on us as we marched. The Drill Sergeant was unphased. Navy Pier is now a park with a huge Ferris wheel and many tourist shops.

As a lark one afternoon, a couple classmates and I cut classes and went to a downtown theater to hear Frank Sinatra sing. He was, by that time, considered one of the most popular singers in America. Elvis Presley was soon to follow. As I recall, Sinatra was accompanied only by a piano. The matinee audience was small, but enthusiastic. Sinatra sang a number of his popular songs. We sang along on the few we knew the lyrics to and applauded loudly. It was a nice break from our studies.

At this time in history, the Korean War was going on. When males reached their 18th birthday, they had to register for the military draft. In the spring of 1953, I received a letter from my Draft Board which was in Memphis. It started out: "Your friends and neighbors have selected you …" So, off I went to fight in the Korean War for Uncle Sam!

A TIME TO SERVE

In June of 1953, my U.S. Army venture began with induction at Fort Sheridan, just north of Chicago. There, I became Private Richard L. Day, U.S. Army, U.S. 55420098. After about two weeks, we were flown to Fort Ord near Monterey, California. This was going to be my home for 16 weeks of combat basic training in preparation for being sent to Korea. My flight to Monterey was in a twin-engine troop carrier. It was a hot, windy, summer day. We bounced all the way from Chicago;

over the Midwest corn and wheat fields to the first fueling stop at Grand Island, Nebraska. During the flight, I threw up every ounce of food I had in my gut. Then, on an empty stomach, I had the dry heaves all the way to the next fueling stop—Salt Lake City. It was far worse than the rides at the Saint Joe County Fair. The stewardess felt so bad for me, that she took me into the airport restaurant, and made me eat a large meal so I had something to empty out again as we continued our flight to Monterey. I began to feel better, and kept the meal down. It was dark and foggy by the time we landed at the Monterey airport. From there we were bussed to Fort Ord. The next day we were issued our uniforms, an M1 rifle, and a footlocker.

Like SMA, the Army was "spit and polish;" but also, a lot of marching, running, physical exercise, weapons instruction, map reading, scrubbing the barracks floors, little sleep, and KP duty (Kitchen Police)—peeling lots of potatoes, and doing lots of dishes, pots and

Breaktime.

Slim and trim.

pans, but eating very well. I was becoming a combat soldier.

Fort Ord rifle range, training with a Browning .30 caliber machine gun.

GOD'S HAND OF PROTECTION

Near the end of our Basic Training, we had an exercise that was supposed to simulate the invasion of a small village. A group of wood-frame buildings had been constructed and arranged along several streets. Our Company of soldiers was spread out in a long line behind three advancing tanks. This was a "live ammo" exercise. We had real bullets in our M1 Garand 30.06 rifles! We were to fire them as we invaded the village. I was a squad leader and had eight men under my command. The plan was for the tanks to lead the advance into the village. Then our long line of squads, spread out behind the tanks, advanced up to the tanks, firing our rifles at the enemy in the village. The sequence continued to repeat itself. My squad was at the very end of the formation. The terrain was hilly sand dunes covered with 8-foot-high brush. As we started the maneuver, I could see the tanks advance and hear the command given to advance. All went well for a while. Due to the hilly terrain, however, I lost visual contact with the rest of our Company. This resulted in my squad being way ahead of where we should have been. Without warning, "bullets" were hitting into the sand around us. I knew we were in big trouble. I yelled to my men to get down and find cover! I knew if anyone was hit, I would be held responsible, and I could see a court martial coming my way. If ever in my life it was time to pray hard it was now. I earnestly called out to God to protect us. He did! "I will be with him in trouble, I will rescue him and honor him" (Psalm 91:15, my paraphrase). Miraculously, no one was hit!

Soon, the rest of the company caught up with us. The strange, but most welcome result was that no one in my squad ever said a word about our experience. We just sort of forgot it. That's the most fear I have ever felt in my lifetime. "As for me, I shall call upon God, and He shall save me" (Psalm 55:16).

ALASKAN WISH

An armistice was signed on July 27th, 1953, and the Korean War fighting ended. The war, however, has yet to be officially declared over. Our basic training ended the following October, and most of my company shipped out to Korea to gather up our wartime materials and ship them back home. I, along with 49 others were sent to special schools at various military installations across America. This assignment took me to Fort Benning, Georgia, where I went to Infantry Sound Ranging School. There were soldiers and officers from many countries attending this school. We were taught how to establish the direction, range, and location of a firing enemy weapon. The sound waves of firing enemy artillery would cross two arrays of geometrically-placed microphones we had set out. This gave us two bearings to the location of the weapon. Where these bearings crossed was the location of the weapon. We called this data to our Fire Direction Center, and they relayed the coordinates to our weapons commanders so then they could fire on the enemy target.

After graduation, we were gathered together and told we could request to be assigned to Europe, Japan, or stateside. I raised my hand and yelled out, "What about Alaska?" The sergeant paused, looked at me for a long time, like I was crazy, and said, "Well, it's not down here, but go ahead and put it down." I then talked six other buddies into requesting an assignment in Alaska instead of Europe or Japan. When the orders were published, all six of us were assigned to Alaska. This came as a big surprise. No one thought we would ever get assigned to Alaska. I took a lot of chiding and verbal abuse from my buddies.

I don't think they ever forgave me. Paris, Berlin, and Tokyo sounded much more appealing than Fairbanks, Alaska. However, this was going to be the fulfillment of the childhood dream I had had since the 9th grade in Memphis. I recall how I used to make a list on a 3x5 card of everything I needed for a big game hunt in Alaska.

My next destination was Fort Lewis, Washington, just outside of Tacoma. I spent Christmas there wandering around downtown Tacoma. The Army could have let us stay home for Christmas, but in typical Army style, that did not happen. In early January of 1954, we boarded a Liberty ship for a very stormy winter voyage to Whittier, Alaska. We pounded through 90-mile an hour wind gusts in the Gulf of Alaska that generated 40-foot waves. All of us Army guys were seasick for most of the three-day voyage. Our bunks were stacked five high and only the top guy could jump out easily. The rest were trapped in their bunk until the guy above you got out of his bunk. Since we were all throwing up, you can imagine the chaos of needing to get up quickly! Our sleeping quarters and the metal grille stairs to the head (bathroom) were slathered and dripping with sour smelling vomit. Of course, the Navy expected us to clean up our mess! Additionally, we were the brunt of all the sailors' jokes.

We arrived in Whittier, Alaska, the night of January 9, 1954. Whittier was, and still is, an ice-free, deep-water port inhabited by only a couple hundred people. Ironically, Sali and I, 54 years later, lived just 20 miles away from Whittier, in the ski resort town of Girdwood.

After a day in Whittier, we were loaded onto a troop train for the long ride to Fairbanks. This was usually about a 15-hour trip. However, due to huge avalanches between Whittier and Anchorage, this was not going to happen. The Alaska Railroad had a specially designed engine with a huge rotary snow plow mounted on the front. Our troop train slowly followed the plow engine through miles of avalanches all the way to Anchorage. Instead of 15 hours, our trip to Fairbanks took two days. It was sunny and minus 35 degrees when we arrived in Fairbanks. I was a very excited 20-year-old just beginning his Alaskan adventure!

LADD AIR FORCE BASE

We were assigned to the Air Force unit at Ladd Field just outside of Fairbanks. Our responsibility was base security. There was a squadron of F-89 jet fighter planes stationed there. At 40 degrees below zero, our huts shook as they took off.

During WWII, planes would be ferried up from Great Falls, Montana to Ladd. There, they were stripped of everything but basic instrumentation and armament. This was to lighten the planes for their flight to Galena or Nome, Alaska, where Russian pilots then flew them

Ladd Field, 1954.

across the Bering Sea to Russia. Many of them didn't make it because there were no navigation aids at that time to help them.

Fighter planes and bombers used in "The Forgotten 1000 Mile War" against the Japanese in the Aleutian Islands, were flown out of Ladd Field. By the end of WWII almost 8,000 planes had been ferried through Ladd Field.

I'm guessing that there were about 3,000 service personnel at Ladd when I was there. Our living quarters, "huts," were officially called James Ways. They were Quonset-like structures, shaped like a half round barrel. The ribbed wooden framework was covered with a heavy black insulated rubber cover. There were six men to a hut. We had a small closet, one table, four chairs and six built-in bunks as furnishings. Pretty spartan I'd say! Our heat was provided by a fuel oil stove.

Army life in peace time is often boring because there was no war to be fought. The enemy is boredom and loss of morale among the troops. This challenges the officers and sergeants with the task of keeping the troops busy with training. So, we always had classes, inspections, maneuvers, guard duty, KP duty, clean up, paint up, fix up, and lots of

PT (physical training). Ask Master Sergeant Richard Harris, Special Forces, my grandson, if it isn't the same today, some 67 years later.

I learned lots about dressing to stay warm at below zero temperatures, how to snowshoe and cross-country ski, and I taught myself to downhill ski at the Birch Hill recreational area. The skis were wooden, with leather strap-on bindings that would not come off when we fell. I had two hard falls which hurt both my knees. I just hobbled around until the swelling went down.

THE ONE-SHOT WAR

I was assigned to "L" Company of the 4th Regimental Combat Team. Four weeks after we arrived in Alaska, our battalion went on a winter maneuver called North Star. We were to be attacked by some paratroopers of the 82nd Airborne from Fort Campbell, Kentucky, as well as additional forces of the 44th Infantry from Fort Lewis, Washington. It was February, and temperatures can be well below zero; so "camping out" in tents was no fun. The only advantage I could think of was—there were NO mosquitoes! We loaded our personal gear into large sleds which were pulled by track vehicles called Weasels. They were World War II vehicles with tired 1947 Studebaker engines in them. Besides Weasels, we had two-and-a-half-ton Dodge trucks for the troops to ride in. Additionally, there were tanks, jeeps, a couple bulldozers, and Otters. Otters were very nice large track vehicles that the officers used.

The troops piled into the insulated back of the two-and-a-half-ton trucks, and off we went to Nenana, (ne nan nah) a small town 50 miles away on the Tanana (tan nah naw) River. There was no road at that time, so our tanks led the way, and we made our own road. If our trucks got stuck, the tanks pulled us out. We spent all day traveling 50 miles and got to Nenana about 7 p.m. The temperature was minus 35 degrees and falling. Then we began the age-old military tradition of waiting … and waiting … for someone higher in rank to make up his mind as to what to do or where to go next? A glorious battle plan had to come forth. The enemy was somewhere in the dark Arctic night creeping up on us. While we waited, fully dressed, and crammed inside the trucks, we argued back and forth about whether to turn the gas heater on or off. The end result was that it got so hot we were sweating; so, we would climb outside to walk around, cool off, and then climb back inside the truck. Meanwhile, the temperature outside dropped to 45 degrees below zero. Finally, at 10:30 p.m., we were given orders to pile out of the warm trucks and start moving down the frozen Tanana River on foot—to find and engage the enemy. It was a still, clear, moonlit night. We could easily read a book by the bright moonlight. It seemed like we could reach out and touch the stars. All this arctic beauty … and yet death was only a misstep away.

As we proceeded down the river, the temperature kept steadily dropping. Some of the troops had on Mukluks, which were good to 65 degrees below zero. They are a type of footgear created by the Eskimos. Ours had a flat leather bottom sewn to a canvas top that tied just below the knee. We put two thick felt soles in them, then a heavy, wool booty, and wore two pairs of wool socks. Great for warmth, but lousy for walking. The felt sole would migrate to one side of the leather bottom and walking was awkward. With no heel it was difficult to walk up or down hill. The rest of the troops, including me, wore insulated, black rubber boots. We called them Mickey Mouse boots because they looked like the cartoon character's footwear. However, they did not breathe like Mukluks. They tended to cause our feet to sweat, and were only good to 35 degrees below zero. Their great advantage was that they had heels and treaded soles—which made them good for walking. Most guys preferred them to Mukluks. The rest of our clothing that night was long johns, heavy wool pants and shirt, field pants, a down-lined field jacket with an attached hood, and two pairs of mittens. The hood had a wolf fur ruff with a bendable wire inside. We bent the wire in the shape of a T-like mouth, which allowed us to see out of the top horizontal bar and breathe through the vertical opening.

The constant danger at such low temperatures was frostbite, which was hard to detect in the moonlight. We had to hold a flashlight on each other's face in order to look for the telltale pale, white spots. Even more dangerous, was freezing our feet and hands. Oh well, we were dumb, happy, and 20 years old.

By 3:30 a.m., the temperature was 63 degrees below zero. We could not find the "enemy," and they could not find us. Actually, I think the Brass realized that an air assault could not be held at these temperatures. The paratroopers would be frozen by the time they hit the ground. Thankfully the maneuver was called off. Our company leader, First Sergeant Johnson, with great exasperation, gave the command to set up our tents. There wasn't an officer in sight. I'll bet they were holed up in their warm Otters!

The difficulty in setting up tents at 63 degrees below zero was that we needed to work without mittens, and we could only stand to be ungloved for about two minutes at a time. Another problem was that at least half of our Weasels had broken down, which left us with 20 guys for every 10-man tent. This led to serious fights to determine who got their sleeping bag closest to the stove. After a 22-hour day, I was exhausted and really looking forward to a good sleep. I slid into my double-down sleeping bag but discovered it was just too cold and I couldn't get to sleep. I finally decided to join a couple buddies sitting around the stove, and we talked through the night. Thankfully, by the next night it had warmed up to 50 degrees below zero, and I could sleep.

During the next day, we wandered around in minus 50-degree temperatures, trying to engage the enemy, and they in turn were trying to find us. We never did see any enemy troops. It was a phantom war with phantom soldiers. Then good fortune shined upon us when a tank parked near us. A bunch of us climbed up onto the back deck exhaust grille to get warm from the engine exhaust. We hadn't been there 10 minutes, when along came one of our slight of stature, bandy-legged, West Point Lieutenants. He couldn't stand for us to have such a warm comfortable roost, and so he commanded us to get off. We stayed put, which enraged him! He finally dislodged us with the threat of a court martial. I think deep down, we knew that nothing that good could last very long. Just then a jet fighter plane flew low over us. We shook our fists and uttered a few oaths because we knew the pilot was going to sleep in a warm bed that night.

I decided to fire my rifle at a large tree stump. I discovered that, at 50 degrees below zero, I could fire only one shot. The bolt came back to pick up another round and stuck there instead of sliding forward to chamber the round. Hence my label for our field maneuvers, "The One-Shot War." About all we proved in the 10-day maneuver was that hand-to-hand combat is not possible at sub zero conditions. There would be no Russian invasion that winter, no Arctic War conducted at 50 degrees below zero.

Vaporizing a cup of water at -50 degrees F.

That first night out, at 63 degrees below zero, caught many guys unprepared, and they suffered severe frostbite. On the second day, many were air evacuated back to the hospital in Fairbanks. I remember visiting them. They had their hands and feet elevated. The frozen flesh was now black, and itched unbearably, yet they couldn't touch their fingers and toes because of the fragility of the frozen tissue. Rumors were out that several troops had frozen to death and one bulldozer had broken through the ice. The present-day Army troops in Alaska don't even consider holding training exercises at temperatures below zero. Wimps!

Mortar platoon at -40 degrees F.

A NASTY CAPTAIN

In the fall of 1954, our new company commander arrived … Captain Sheppard. He was a Texas A & M graduate, probably in his late-40s, whom I would describe as wiry, crew cut, and unfriendly—with nary a smile ever crossing his face.

We had Reveille every weekday morning at 6:30 a.m. The O.C. (Officer in Charge) went from hut to hut and awakened the troops. We assembled for a brief roll call during which all troops were accounted for. Then, we ran to the mess hall for breakfast. The O.C., on one particular morning, was Sergeant Olson. He did not come to my hut and give a shout, so I missed Reveille. The ranking person is the one who takes charge of the platoon, and in my case, that was Corporal Stafford. He had studied for the priesthood, and was a reasonable guy, but totally out of place as an Infantry Combat Soldier. The troops formed right outside my hut. I could have reached through the wall and touched the guys in the back row. Corporal Stafford had been in my hut and knew where I was.

I was awakened by the sound of troops running alongside my hut to the mess hall. I leaped out of bed, threw my clothes on, and ran to the mess hall. Some of my buddies immediately told me that Stafford had reported me as absent. I quickly found Sergeant Olson who was having coffee with other sergeants. I told him: "I wasn't absent—no one woke me up!" Then he casually said, "Yah, yah," like … okay, I believe you. So, I thought all was well.

My hut was composed of headquarters personnel. I was a mail and supply clerk. There was a baker, who got up at 2 a.m.; the company clerk, who got up a half hour before the troops so he could type his daily report; a baseball player, who had the day off, so I was the only person who had to get up for Reveille. My guess was that Sergeant Olson figured that no one in our hut had to get up so he just passed by. However, he would never admit it!

A couple hours later, the company clerk, Corporal Ralson Rhodes, came storming up to me—complaining that I had caused him an undue amount of grief! "How so?" I questioned him. He said that he had to type up, in triplicate, a multiple-page "Article 15," which Captain Sheppard was going to give me for missing Reveille. An "Article 15" is a disciplinary measure, short of a court-martial, to punish one *for various infractions of military rules. I was to be confined to the base for the weekend and put on KP* duty for that time. I was soon ordered to the captain's office. I stood before the captain's desk at stiff attention, trembling inside and near tears. He told me that he was issuing me an "Article 15" because I missed Reveille. I told him that Sergeant Olson did not wake me. His reply was that Sergeant Olson said that he did wake all huts, and he believed the sergeant. I told Captain Sheppard that I didn't think I deserved an "Article 15" — that it wasn't fair! This angered the captain. I probably should have kept my mouth shut. Captain Sheppard said that he would talk to Sergeant Olson again, and he dismissed me.

I went back to my hut feeling angry and cheated—waiting for the next order. Out of helpless frustration, I punched the insulated sides of the hut until my knuckles bled! Sergeant McGowan, my platoon sergeant, and company Master Sergeant Robertson, came to my hut to hear my side of the story. They believed me and went to bat for me. Down deep inside I had this hunch that our new company commander wanted to put the fear of God into the "L" Company troops, and I was to be made an example—the "scapegoat" of his stern and absolute authority over us. I felt I was a good trooper. I did as I was ordered and was never in any sort of trouble. I faded into the wall paper as much as I could, an old Army tactic we all seemed to learn—never raise your hand to volunteer for anything. The Army at that time was a draft Army, not a volunteer organization. This meant that most soldiers were there by order and not by choice. The result was, every unit had its share of "goof-offs," guys who had minimal education and were very unhappy with having to spend two years of their lives in the service of their country. Their attitude and effort showed it. I think the captain thought—by punishing me, for a minor infraction, he would put all the "goof-off" troops under his command on notice. If they stepped out of line, they could expect to get whacked by a big stick!

Ralson Rhodes showed up about an hour later, anxiously puffing away on his cigarette, and very upset because he heard that Captain Sheppard was now considering putting me up for a Summary Court Martial instead of an "Article 15." From Ralson's unhappy view, he faced a month of having to type volumes of court martial documents perfect and in triplicate.

Soon after that, I was again ordered to appear before the captain. I stood, in my Class A uniform, at stiff attention before Captain Sheppard's desk. My heart was pounding; the sweat beads were popping out on my forehead. The captain was steaming mad. He said that he wanted to put me up for a court martial even though he thought the case would probably be thrown out of court. It didn't matter to him whether or not anyone had woken me; this was the Army! I was expected to be present at Reveille formation regardless of the circumstance! Through clenched teeth, he said that because Sergeant Robertson and Sergeant McGowan had spoken in my favor; he was dropping the "Article 15." Then he paused; and with emphasis, he said to me: "Never, under any circumstance, do I ever want to see you in my office again!" I was dismissed. I was happy. Sergeants Robertson and McGowan were happy. And happiest of all, was Corporal Ralson Rhodes the "L" Company clerk. "God is a shield to all who trust in him" (Psalm 18:30 — my paraphrase).

BASKETBALL REDEMPTION

A notice was posted on the company bulletin board encouraging each company to form a basketball team to play in a Battalion League. I was a fair basketball player, but I was not a coach or organizer. However, I thought, "What the heck, I'll give it a try."

I put the word out that I was forming an "L" Company basketball team. There were only eight or 10 guys who showed up for the first practice. We were a real "rag tag" group. I didn't think we stood a chance to win even one game. The first game was scheduled, and we won. The second game came along, and we won again. Then, we miraculously won the third game. With overwhelming odds against us, we went on to win the Battalion Championship and a decent-sized trophy. I think, by this time, everyone on the team believed in the providence of God. I sure did. He must have either made the ball smaller or the rim larger for each of our shots! Keep in mind that Captain Sheppard must surely have been aware that his company team had been winning basketball games.

Next came the Regimental Basketball Championship Tournament! Bless Captain Sheppard's little Grinch heart … on a bitter cold, and gray November day, he marched all of "L" Company a mile and a half to watch our tournament game. This was a "David versus Goliath" game; sorta like little Colon High versus The University of Michigan. Sorry, no miracle happened; we were beaten handily. I had no idea what our small and inexperienced ball team could accomplish. We far exceeded any hope that I ever had imagined.

A week later, First Sergeant Robertson asked me (actually, ordered me) to present Captain Sheppard with the trophy we had won as Battalion Champs. I felt this would be an extremely awkward meeting, but had no way to get out of it. Sergeant Robertson arranged the meeting. On the day of the meeting, I made sure my uniform was perfect, shined my shoes and brass, even shined the trophy; spit and polish all the way! Sergeant Robertson ushered me into Captain Sheppard's office. I stood at rigid attention as team captain. Sergeant Robertson explained to the Captain how we had won the Battalion Basketball Championship, and I was there to present the captain our Battalion Basketball Championship trophy. He was pleased to receive it and was gracious in his acceptance. I silently recalled how a couple months before he had said that, "I never want, under ANY circumstance, to see you in my office again!"

*My granddaughter, Linnea, and me on
my Honor Flight to Washington, DC.*

*Sgt. Harris—combat-ready
in Afghanistan.*

*My grandson, Army Special Forces
Sergeant Rich Harris, receiving his Silver
Star, the third-highest medal of honor for
valor in combat.*

GO BLUE TIME

A DREAM COME TRUE

In May of 1955, I finished my Alaskan tour of duty and was transferred back to Ft. Sheridan where I had begun my military duty a couple years earlier. I spent two boring weeks hanging around the barracks waiting to be discharged. The Army seemed determined to squeeze every last day I owed out of me. A sergeant in the records department offered me a cash bonus of $300 and a sergeant's rank to reenlist. Thanks, but no thanks. It was time to go back to college. This time I wanted to fulfill my dream to attend the University of Michigan in Ann Arbor. I was interviewed by the University Engineering School dean. Because I was not a resident of Michigan, he recommended that I work for six months and then enroll as a Michigan resident. This would stretch out my G.I. Bill funds also. I got a job working for the Ford Motor Company in Ypsilanti. They assigned me to the Horn Testing Department; "Beep, boop, bop; beep, boop, bop"; enough to drive one nuts! Fortunately, they had us change jobs every couple hours. I learned that I did not like assembly line work. In January of 1956, I was accepted at the University of Michigan and enrolled in Civil Engineering School. It was academically hard, and I had to burn the midnight oil to keep up with my studies, but I loved being a student at Michigan.

AN ELVIS DIGRESSION

While in the Army, I corresponded with Sandra, the sister of a girl friend from Central High School in Memphis. She invited me to come down to Memphis to take her to her Tech High School prom. My Aunt Helen, my mother's sister, lived in Memphis, and I could stay at her home. I caught a Greyhound Bus in Detroit and made the long trip. On prom night, I borrowed my Uncle Nelson's car to take Sandra to her prom. We headed for a downtown hotel named the Gayoso. Parked right in front of the hotel was a beautiful baby-pink Cadillac convertible. As we entered the hotel lobby there was a bunch of the graduating class and their dates all gathered around another couple. We went to see what the commotion was about. There, sitting on a couch, was my date's classmate with her date—Elvis Presley. This was June of 1956. Elvis was well known in the South, but not nationally. That fame came in the next couple years. He was well dressed and very cordial to all of us. Everyone was greeting him and shaking his hand. Now I knew the owner of that Cadillac convertible. That's all I remember about the night. Life is full of amazing and unusual circumstances.

JIMMY HOFFA

Although I had the G.I. Bill to help fund my education, I always tried to find a summer job. My dad was running his last truck line, Ellis Trucking, in Dearborn, Michigan. He offered me a job on the dock, loading trucks with the night crew. All the dock hands, mechanics, and drivers were Teamster Union members. Their President was the notorious Jimmy Hoffa. The reputation of Hoffa and the Teamster leadership was not what we might term, "highly ethical or honest." It was not unusual for them to be connected with organized crime, fraud, and bribery. The only reason I got the job was that I was the boss's son, not a Teamster member, so therefore a "Scab." The dock hands treated me with respect, and I was able to keep up with them loading the trucks. About every two weeks, a big limo pulled up into the yard. The Teamster cadre piled out, and they and the dock hands had a meeting or gripe session. I was persona non grata, and was ordered to go hide up in one of the trailers until the meeting was over.

My father had related to me that the dock hands were stealing tires, pharmaceuticals, batteries, and Browning Shotguns. He was very angry about this situation and struggled to resolve it. I remember him saying that he'd have to have five witnesses of one of the dock hands killing someone before he could fire him! I also knew that if Jimmy Hoffa ever came to one of the Teamster dock meetings, my dad, O.B. Day, all 5'8" of him, would confront him.

One evening the limo pulled up and Jimmy Hoffa stepped out. Dad was still in his office and obviously observed this. As Hoffa and his men climbed up on the dock, I was ordered to hide in one of the trailers. I was able to position myself in the trailer, out of sight, but still where I could peek through a crack in the door and see what was going on.

Sure enough, my hunch was right! As Hoffa and the dock workers were having their meeting, my dad came out on the dock and confronted Hoffa about his Teamsters stealing freight. It was a loud and nasty conversation. The air around them was blue with anger! O.B. Day had his say, turned, and went back into his office. I scooted up into the front of the trailer so as not to be caught watching. Years later Jimmy Hoffa was murdered; they're still trying to find where he's buried.

A SPECIAL MICHIGAN COED

In October,1956, I was in my sophomore year in Civil Engineering. It was one of those beautiful Michigan fall days ... I was walking from the Engineering School to my car when I noticed this good looking, knock out girl, standing at a Student Body Election voting table. I walked on by, but I could not get the girl out of my mind. The further I got from the voting table the stronger the urge to return! I thought, well, if I go back and vote, maybe somehow, I could get her phone number. So back to the voting table I went. I handed my student ID to the unknown miss and voted. When she returned my ID, I said, "Does your phone number go with the ballot?" She gave me a coy smile, sort of danced around, and said "Mais non, Monsieur." (*But no, sir.*) As I walked back to my car, I determined in my mind that somehow I had to meet this girl. I drove slowly back toward the voting table and saw that a University truck had picked up the table. The girl and the guy who had been attending the table with her, were walking toward the Engineering School Arch. I drove ahead of them, parked my car and followed behind at a safe distance—007 in action! They slowly walked across campus and finally wound up at Vicky Vaughn, a women's dorm. I stood peering through the corner windows of a restaurant which was downhill and across the street from them. They continued talking on and on ... . How long was this going to take? I was getting cold and realized that once this girl got into the dorm and out of sight, I would not be able to talk to her. It was time for me to do something! I turned up my coat collar to cover my face, crossed the street, and walked quickly past them, into the dorm entry.

Eventually, my dream girl came into the dorm and I was able to intercept her and introduce myself. I said: "My name is Dick Day, I'm 23. I'm an engineering student, and an ATO pledge, and could I have your phone number, please?" We chatted briefly, and she somewhat reluctantly gave me her name and phone number. I was elated and very much looked forward to asking her out for a date.

That's how I first met my wife, Sally, now Sali—her arty spelling. I didn't waste any time, and called her for a dinner date, to which she agreed. I picked her up at 7 p.m., and we drove to Ypsilanti, about seven miles away, for pizza. The evening was going great for about a couple bites of pizza—at which point Sali announced that she had "late minutes" and had to be back to the dorm by 8 p.m. That quickly ended a lovely evening as we had to hurry back to Vicky Vaughn. "Late minutes" were given out as punishment for not being back to her dorm by curfew hour. Here I am, out on my first date with this beautiful girl that I had worked so hard to meet, and she was being disciplined for getting in late from a date with another guy. It turned out that she was dating some "obvious clod" who didn't get her back to the dorm on time. We had only three

Sali, the co-ed I chased since 1957!

dates that school year. C'est la vie. We miraculously wrote each other a letter a summer later and reestablished contact. She was then attending Michigan State University, and I would drive up into "enemy territory" to see her or bring her to Ann Arbor for some fraternity function or a football game. Don't worry, I wasn't going to let this girl get away.

ANOTHER RUDY STORY

I think a lot of guys dream about a sort of *RUDY* story in their life ... so here's mine. High school football was my favorite sport. Of course, it was a kid's dream of mine to play football for the University of Michigan.

I had been in Civil Engineering School since January of 1956. In April, 1957, I somehow found out that spring football practice was open to "walk-ons." This meant we did not have to have a scholarship to play.

I was overloaded with courses such as physics, calculus, economics, and engineering school courses—consequently I didn't have three extra hours a day in which to practice football. However, I decided—what the heck! Nothing ventured, nothing gained.

Go Blue!

I went to the athletic department and talked to coach Don Dufek. Coach Dufek had been selected All American in 1955 and MVP of the Rose Bowl game. His thigh muscle expansion was so great that it split the seams of his canvas practice pants. I would not have liked trying to tackle him! He then said to me to just go ahead and draw out my gear, and then show up for practice.

So, I headed for the equipment room. As I approached the entry, there was a tall guy standing with his arm stretched across the doorway. I just walked under his arm and turned around to see who he was. Michigan had two All American ends that year, and there stood one of them—Ron Kramer. Suddenly, spring practice didn't seem like such a good idea. I couldn't see myself playing against someone a hundred pounds heavier and a foot taller than me. In spite of that, I drew out my equipment and said to myself, "No guts. No glory."

The following year, Ron Kramer was drafted by the Green Bay Packers. He played for them for seven years.

On the practice field, we non-scholarship guys were the "red shirts" and played mostly defense. We were basically cannon fodder for the varsity to pummel. I loved defense and played middle linebacker. Tackling a 225 pound fullback was a maximum effort for me. I weighed about 169 pounds wringing wet. For the three weeks of practice, I was black and blue with bruises. I felt like one big piece of hamburger. Actually, I WAS one big piece of hamburger. My grades were also turning into hamburger.

At the end of the three weeks of spring practice, we went into The Big House to play a regulation game. We had Big Ten referees, and it was open to the public. There was no marching band or cheerleaders, but I would get to run through the stadium tunnel and play in this famous, historic stadium. The Varsity scholarship boys were the "blue shirts," and the non-scholarship guys became the "white shirts." There were roughly 3000 or 4000 fans in the stadium. Our ragtag, second string, walk-on team was fired up; adrenalin was flowing at a high level. We had no scholarship to lose, and no reason to hold anything back. We just played our hearts out, gave it our best effort, and left all we had to give on the field. That we did, that we did. The final score of the game was 25 to 12. We had won the game. The Varsity team, the mighty Goliath, had fallen. We were ecstatic.

It was tradition that the "Blues" win this game. Coach Bennie Oosterbaan was ticked-off. He was a former All-American end for Michigan. This was his last year to coach and he couldn't stand for the "pipsqueak" walk-on, non-scholarship team to beat his Varsity boys. He insisted that the game be extended for another quarter, with no time limit, so the Varsity could beat us. We had no bench strength to draw on. We had defeated them fair and square and had nothing else to prove. The second, final score, after a very long fifth quarter, was 31-25. The next day, Sunday, May 12, 1957, in the Detroit Sunday Times sports section was the story, "Reserves Tough for UM Blues." There was only one picture with the article. It was of me defending against a touchdown pass. I still have the article. It's a little tattered, torn, and yellowing with age, but still a record of my "Rudy Story."

Years later, the summer of 2003, I wrote to the Michigan football coach, Lloyd Carr, and told him the story. I sent him a copy of the article and made one request: Could he get me four tickets to the Michigan-Ohio State football game that following November? I received a call from Coach Carr's secretary saying the tickets were available.

Sali and I flew to Grand Rapids from Alaska and had our grandsons Justin and Jordan Janowski, fly over from Milwaukee. They were on the Mukwonago, Wisconsin, High School football team that won the Wisconsin State Football Championship the following year.

We all stayed the night at the lovely home of Sali's sister and her husband, Judy and Elden Stielstra. We were treated to one of Judy's great dinners, ending with one of her delicious pies.

On the Friday before the game, I drove the four of us to Ann Arbor and we stayed in a motel near the city. The next morning, Game Day, was a typical November Ann Arbor day; cold, cloudy, windy, and rainy.

We headed for the stadium. After parking, we had a long way to walk. The clouds began to clear … and a ray or two of sunshine peeked through. We checked out the tailgate parties going on near the stadium and then went into The Big House well before kickoff to watch all the pageantry.

Our seats were in the end zone corner about 25 rows up, with a good view of all the action at our end of the field. By kick off time, to our great delight, the sun was out

Sali in the Big House.

and it was a glorious fall day. The band performed, the cheerleaders did their acrobatic routines, and the mighty Michigan Wolverines beat The Ohio State Buckeyes, 35-21 before 112,118 fans. I was so elated that our grandsons had seen Michigan play and win in The Big House where their grandfather had played his one victorious college football game. That was a glorious day in my life—in all of our lives.

CLAVEY RIVER BRIDGE

In the summer of 1957, I found a job in the Stanislaus National Forest near Sonora, California. An engineering school classmate, Bryson McBratney, offered me a ride to Los Angeles. Bryson was a former Marine. He was struggling academically and wanted to return home for a fresh start. He and his wife, their two children, and I piled into his new Ford Fairlane and drove nonstop down the famous "Route 66" to Los Angeles in 48 hours. We got one speeding ticket in Albuquerque, and stopped for only one two-hour nap. I had no knowledge of Los Angeles neighborhoods, and Bryson had never said a word about his family. We turned into a neighborhood called Bel Air. It was graced with lush vegetation and mansions. Bryson looked at me and laughed, as we pulled into the driveway of a home bigger and more beautiful than I had ever seen.

Bel Air is in the foothills of the Santa Monica Mountains. The residents include many celebrities and movie stars. I was ensconced in the maid's quarters for a few days and treated like a special guest. After a three-day stay, because of my independent nature, and not wanting to wear out my welcome, I found a room in Venice, a Bohemian-spirited, Pacific beach community. I was totally unaware of the notoriety and character of where I was now going to lay down my head and sleep for the night.

I had shared my California plans with Jerry—(I can't remember his last name), another engineering school classmate. He had given me his father's phone number in Berkeley and said to contact him if I was looking for a job. After a couple days in Venice, I called the Berkeley number and explained to Jerry's father, who worked for the U.S. Forest

Service, that I was looking for a summer job. As God promises: "Ask and you will receive." Jerry's father said he had connections with the Supervisor of the Stanislaus National Forest and he was sure that there was a job waiting for me.

So, my trail led from Ann Arbor, down Highway 66, to a millionaire mansion, to a Bohemian enclave, and now to a construction camp in the Stanislaus Forest. "One never knows, does one?" Encouraged by the prospect of a job, I hitchhiked from L.A. to San Francisco where I passed by my Army Basic Training Base at Fort Ord. So many memories began flashing through my mind, weeks on the rifle range, KP duty, midnight marches, guard duty, spit and polish inspections, all in preparation for combat duty in Korea. Thankfully, that never came to pass.

Jerry's father picked me up in his restored Model A Ford Coupe and took me on a tour of the University of California, Berkley campus. He then gave me a "hands-on" fly-tying and knot-tying lesson, and loaned me a fly rod and reel so that I could fish for trout in the Stanislaus streams.

I took a bus from San Francisco to Sonora and reported to the forest supervisor. My two years of civil engineering qualified me to be the engineer on a logging bridge project on the Clavey River. This seemed to be way over my head, but the primary requirement was to be able to handle a surveyor's transit, which I learned to do in my surveying courses. If the forest supervisor thought I could handle the job, then I guessed he knew he could trust me to do the job. I had no idea what I was getting into… seems like the theme of this whole trip!

The next morning, Grady, a good ole' Southern Boy, picked me up in a red Dodge half-ton pickup for the long ride back into the Stanislaus Forest to the construction camp.

I should tell you about the colorful history of the Sonora, California, area. Sonora and the Stanislaus Forest are in the foothills of the Sierra Nevada Mountains, just east of Sacramento. The area gained its fame primarily from the discovery of gold in about 1849. The professional football team, "San Francisco 49ers" takes its name from this discovery.

Black Bart, an Englishman, was a notorious Wells Fargo stagecoach robber in the area at that time. Mark Twain, who is famous for his Mississippi River stories of Huckleberry Finn and Tom Sawyer, actually got his start in this area. He overheard a story in a bar in nearby Angels Camp that led to his writing *The Jumping Frog of Calaveras County*. This story was his first great success as a writer and brought him national attention. The town of Angels Camp, even to this day, has a jumping frog contest. You can even rent a frog to enter and win as much as $5000. The record jump is close to 21 feet. What a frog! Another famous author from this area was Bret Harte. Hence the town named Twain Harte.

The restaurant in Sonora where I went for breakfast, was frequented by the movie and TV actor, Dale Robertson. He was doing a TV series in the area. I usually had coffee and pancakes, which cost me 35 cents. I wondered if Robertson had a similar budget? My budget for daily eating was $2.00. In 1957 that was possible.

Grady and I bounced along a very winding gravel road, going deeper and deeper into the Stanislaus Forest. We came to a shady, sharp turn where there was a trickle of a stream coming down from an adjacent bank. I'm kind of just observing the flora and fauna … when there, right before my eyes … was a big rattlesnake getting a drink. I yelled to Grady, "Stop the truck!" He slammed on the brakes. I jumped out, and quickly found a round, discus-like rock, with a sharp edge. You know the kind you want to skip on water. I scooted around the truck to where I could make a good throw. I gave the rock a heave and miraculously almost cut the rattler in half. His death was instant. He was a large snake, at least three feet long. I tossed him into the back of the truck and Grady and I continued on to the camp. Our conversation was all about the rattler and what a lucky kill I had made.

When we got to the camp, I met my boss, Connie Chung, a very gregarious Chinese guy, whom I liked immediately. All the construction crew loved the snake story, which Grady seemed to love to tell, adding his own embellishments. I skinned the snake and cut it into four inch pieces. The meat was white, very similar to chicken meat. With a little help from the cook, I fried up the pieces, only to find out that although the taste was good, it was too tough to chew. Well, it was worth a try. Not a single construction crew member offered to give it a taste. C'est la vie.

I found a recipe of kerosene and Ivory soap to use to tan the snake skin. That actually worked pretty well. I wanted to make a belt out of the skin, but I have no idea where that snake skin wound up.

For the next four weeks, I worked along with the bridge crew. They were building the forms for the two 25-foot columns that would support the bridge deck over the Clavey River. The river was about 15 to 20 feet wide where we were building the bridge. The water was crystal clear and we could see beautiful trout swimming above and below where we worked. Plus, the swimming was great!

My real job didn't begin until we began pouring the concrete for the columns and end footings. There were four 30-foot I-beams at each end of the bridge and three 50-foot I-beams that spanned the river from column to column. The vertical part of the I-beam was called the "web," and the upper and lower horizontal parts are called the "flanges." At each end, and on both sides of the lower flange, that rested on the concrete end footer and column, were holes for large threaded studs. The studs enabled us to bolt the I-beams down. It was my responsibility to position the threaded studs in the final concrete pour. My room for error was at most a half inch in any direction. There was a huge lump in my throat as I peered through my transit, and I called out the line and position of the studs. The workmen followed my instructions as they sank the studs into the wet concrete and fastened them to a template that held them in position while the concrete set. Connie said we should let the concrete cure for at least 36 hours before setting the beams.

The next day the crew was gathering all the materials ready to build the deck that the I-beams supported. I set up my transit and went over the measurements that I had used to position the threaded studs, now firmly set in concrete. No adjustments could be made, it was what it was. My boss, Connie, went through my measurements with me and seemed satisfied that I was correct. Tomorrow was the big day!

I didn't sleep a wink that night. I kept going over and over all my math and transit work to locate the threaded studs in the column tops. Morning couldn't come soon enough. The whole crew knew that I was sweating out this day. Connie was directing the whole show. He positioned several men where each end of the beam would be attached. Their job was to guide the beams into place and bolt them down. The shorter 30-foot beams at one end of the bridge went into place with no problems. Now it was time to set the long 60-foot beams. The crane operator climbed up into the crane cab and fired up the diesel engine. Then he swung the boom over to where the beams were stacked and lowered the cable and harness. His helper secured the first beam for the lift. Each beam weighed about 6,700 pounds. I stood nearby and watched all the action, praying to God that I had made no mistakes on my first bridge. What did I know about building bridges … not very much.

The crane operator gave me a smile and a thumbs up as he tightened the cable and lifted the beam. He had to slowly swing it in an arc over the river and then drop it down to where the crew could grab the ends and bring it into position for lowering it over the studs. My heart pounded, and I was close to tears as the beam was slowly dropped into place. Now the guys at each end of the beam guided the holes in the flange over the protruding studs. On signal of the crew, the crane operator dropped the beam, inch by inch, to seat it over the protruding studs. All

seemed to be going well. Then one of the crew at the end of the beam gave out a big WHOOP! Everyone chimed in, someone's hat went into the river, and a brief celebration ensued. We were a happy bunch of bridge builders out in the Stanislaus Forest. I got congratulations, pats on the back, handshakes, and Connie had enthusiastic words of encouragement. The second and third beams were lifted and dropped into place—a perfect fit. The camp dinner that night was cheerful, with a few extra beers opened. Even the cook was happy. Thank you Lord for this successful day. Oh, yes. I slept well that night. Go Blue!

CHANGING DIRECTION

By my junior year my interest in civil engineering started to wane. So, I began to search around for some other academic direction. I went to Rackham Graduate School and took a battery of tests which only confirmed what I already knew, that I was strong in math and science. Somewhere, back in the archives of my memory, was an experience I had had in the ninth grade, when I went to the University of Tennessee Dental School in Memphis for dental care. My student dentist had been in the Army in WWII. He was a very likable guy and explained each procedure to me as he went along. The imprint of those dental appointments stayed with me and must have contributed to my deciding to apply to Michigan Dental School. The dean of the dental school, Dr. Robert Doerr, interviewed me. He went through all my Civil Engineering School courses and gave me credit for them all for entry into dental school. Hindsight tells me that my Honorable Discharge from the Army was a strong factor in my favor. The only additional requirements were to take organic chemistry and biology. I had no trouble with the biology course, but organic chemistry was a different story.

My first experience with chemistry was my senior year at Sewanee. Our chemistry teacher was Colonel Moore. We called him "Colonel Piddle Moore." He was a good teacher and didn't deserve the chiding. Of course, we didn't tell him our little joke. Boys will be boys! Our class seemed to be determined to do dumb things, ask dumb questions and learn very little. I never achieved a good understanding of acids, bases, mole, pH, etc. I did well in the laboratory experiments but struggled with the lecture material and exams. I was glad to get my C in the course and say goodbye to chemistry. Good riddance, I thought. I'll never have to crack a chemistry text again!

Five years later, I was faced with the requirement of taking an organic chemistry course as a requirement to enter dental school. I could handle calculus, physics, economics, biology, trigonometry, but chemistry? Ugh. Organic chemistry was a five hour course that required an enormous amount of study time and additional laboratory time. I did well in the lab, but got a D in lecture. This put me on shaky ground as far as acceptance into dental school. I went, again, to the dean of the dental school, to ask him what my status was. He said I would have to retake the lecture class during the summer, and not only pass, but get a B in order to be accepted into dental school.

This put an enormous amount of pressure on me. I was living at my parent's townhouse on the west side of Detroit, so I had to drive 35 miles into Ann Arbor three times a week to attend the lectures. I went to the ATO fraternity house, and in their exam file, found five old Organic exams–one for every exam I had to take that summer. I poured over my lecture notes and memorized the old exam question answers and miraculously got my "B"!

Some 65 years later my research shows me that Organic Chemistry is a "make or break" course for entering medical or dental school. It is also one of the most difficult of all college courses. One of the difficulties of the course is that it's considered to be unintuitive and half of the students who take the course drop out. I can only conclude that God miraculously interceded for me in getting a "B" in Organic. Also another summer miracle was that I miraculously reconnected, via letters, with Sali.

So, in September of 1958, I started dental school in the "Famous" Class of 62. I've learned that every class thinks they're famous. Many of the class members had other degrees, and several were married with children. Our ages were from 22 to 40 years old. There were 100 students in my class—all males. Women now make up about 50 percent of the dental classes. Seventy-five members of my class graduated; which means, 25 percent failed or dropped out. This was a very painful and disappointing experience for those who had their hearts set on becoming a dentist. It was especially hard if their father was a dentist.

A sudden, sad experience disrupted our young lives. The day we finished our final exams as juniors, we went to the Pretzel Bell for a few beers and pizza celebration. Most of us, because of long hours of studying, "cramming," were extremely short on sleep. One classmate,

Nick, left the Bell, picked up his belongings, and took off in his VW Bug for home in Detroit. With too much beer, on top of no sleep for three days, Nick headed down the "off ramp" onto I-94, right into the oncoming traffic. We all wept and grieved over the loss of his life.

A BIOCHEMICAL NIGHTMARE

My next chemical encounter occurred the second semester of my freshman year in dental school—biochemistry, a required course. At the time, I was often driving 65 miles to the Michigan State campus where Sali had enrolled. Our relationship was blossoming and I had to make time to spend with her. She was the love of my life and marriage was on the horizon. As far as chemistry, it was the same old story; I aced the laboratory part and got a D in lecture. This was in May, 1959. The dental school now required me to retake the final exam in September and get at least a B in order to continue as a sophomore with my class. I discussed this with my chemistry professor, Dr. Harvey Weinstein, and he said to come back in September and retake the exam.

HOT WEDDING ... HONEYMOON BLUES

Sali and I set the date for our summer wedding, August 29, 1959, at Saint Mark's Cathedral in Grand Rapids, Michigan. My mother-in-law, Beatrice, bless her heart, planned every aspect of our formal wedding. My beautiful bride was escorted down the aisle by her Great-uncle Carl, as her father had died in an auto accident when she was seven years old. The temperature that day was 98 degrees with no air conditioning in the cathedral or reception hall! I was perspiring and soaking my tux and Sali's curls had melted.

After our promises, before God and man—to love and to cherish, till death do us part, and our "I do's" ... our reception was held in the Cathedral Fellowship Hall.

Following the reception with family and friends, we drove north to Epworth Heights for the beginning of our honeymoon. Epworth is a

Methodist summer campground, just outside of Ludington, Michigan, Sali's birth place. We stayed in the beautiful Epworth Hotel and had a lovely room overlooking Lake Michigan.

"Sally" and Dick.
Our first marriage.

The next day we headed for Mackinac (Mackinaw) Island to stay at the Grand Hotel. No cars were allowed on the island, but they offered tours by horse-drawn "Surreys With The Fringe On Top." Surely, I was going to treat my bride to this unique tour. The surrey had four rows of seats that held 16 people and was pulled by two large draft horses.

As we were ready to board the surrey, another couple pushed past us to take the front seats. This put them on either side of the driver who was perched up higher in a separate seat. The husband was behind one horse, and the wife behind the other. I need to mention that the Mrs. was heavily made up with lots of deep red lipstick, heavy mascara, and dark eyebrow pencil. Also, she evidently partook of significant amounts of high-calorie food items.

Off we went. "Giddyup, Buster. Giddyup, Duke." We trotted along on a cobblestone road as our driver pointed out the various landmarks of interest. Unfortunately, our route had several small hills for Buster and Duke to climb. I say "unfortunately," because on every hill, Buster audibly emitted methane gas. The Mrs. had chosen the seat which placed her right behind Buster's derrière. Following Buster's unseemly behavior, she pursed her lips, squinched her eyes closed, and turned her head to the left and then to the right, to avoid the blast. We couldn't keep from laughing … into our cupped hands of course. Our laughter and tears flowed on every hill.

After a couple of fun days, since the weather was cold and rainy on Mackinac Island, we were happy to drive back to Ludington, where we stayed in an upstairs apartment at Sali's grandparents' home. We were only a couple blocks from beautiful Lake Michigan, where a lighthouse and breakwater created the harbor entrance for car ferries.

Honeymoons, of course, should be all love, joy, and laughter. However, real life tends to sneak in. Oh, come on now, you know I'm telling the truth. We had planned to go perch fishing the next morning at 4 a.m., and sweet, innocent, Dickey Day jumped out of bed … but Sali could not. So, I left my new bride behind and went perch fishing out on the breakwater alone. I would quickly learn that sunrise is not Sali's favorite time for any kind of activity, not even fishing, which she loves to do.

My perch fishing led me to my first visit in the marital doghouse, which has had several pairs of worn out hinges replaced over the last 60 years. Unbeknownst to me, Sali kept her disappointment to herself for years—until the writing of this book—that I preferred to go fishing by myself instead of staying in bed with her on our honeymoon. Sali reminded me too, that the perch weren't biting and I was skunked! This leads me to share with you my definition of marriage, learned through trial and error: "Marriage … a state of continual forgiveness by both husband and wife." Scripture admonishes us, "And be kind to one another, tender hearted, forgiving one another, even as God in Christ forgave you" (Ephesians 4:32).

A BIOCHEMISTRY MIRACLE

The date of my biochemistry exam was about two weeks later—after our honeymoon and the wedding of a fraternity brother in Bay City. Great! Just great! Needless to say, I took my biochemistry book and notes on our honeymoon and then to the wedding. My having to study and memorize chemical formulas put a damper on our time in Ludington. Sali had looked forward to swimming in Lake Michigan and enjoying the beautiful sunshine and sandy beach. Being confined to our small apartment was not her idea of honeymoon fun. Then, while we were staying in the Bay City area for my fraternity brother's wedding, I remember sitting alongside a country road adjacent to a corn field, with Sali sunning herself, and me, pouring over my biochemistry notes.

After my fraternity brother's wedding, Sali and I drove to Ypsilanti and settled into our little trailer home. The time now had come for me to retake my Biochem final exam. I drove into Ann Arbor and reported to Professor Weinstein at the medical school. We exchanged pleasantries, and he asked me how my summer was. I told him that I had just gotten married two weeks ago. A long period of silence ensued, and then Dr.Weinstein raised both hands and dramatically exclaimed: "What!?! You mean to tell me that you have been studying for this exam on your honeymoon?"

"Yes," I replied. He sat down at his desk, held his head with both hands, and said: "You are not ready to take this exam. I'll give you permission to continue with your class and then I expect you to come back here at Christmas time and take the exam. Is that agreeable?" This was more than agreeable to me, but it got even better. Dr. Weinstein handed me several sheets of paper and said "Here's the exam. Come back at Christmas, take the exam, and do NOT get an A". I left the room rejoicing. I could not hold back the tears. "Thank you, God, thank you God!"

Needless to say, I took the exam during Christmas vacation and avoided getting an "A," settling for the required "B." To show my appreciation I brought along a Christmas card and a bottle of Jack Daniels for Dr. Weinstein, hoping my Jewish professor would accept them from a very thankful, lowly dental student. Dr.Weinstein graciously, and with humorous comments about being bribed, accepted my gift. It was another great day in my life.

Chemistry courses and chemistry exams were over for me, forever. Hallelujah! Aspirin and Ibuprofen were as close to chemistry as I ever needed to get. Each time that there was a hard struggle … then a failure; each time there appeared the possibility of redemption … and resurrection. With every failure, there was the chance to try again … to not give up, but to go on, to jump one more hurdle … to succeed where I had previously failed. Remember this life lesson when things seem bleak and hopeless; determine to persevere, to keep pressing on. "Though a good man may fall seven times, he is soon up again"

(Proverbs 24:16 — my paraphrase). And "I can do all things through Christ who strengthens me" (Philippians 4:13).

The life of a dental student is a very busy one. Most of us were married and had children. While I was attending dental school in Ann Arbor, Sali was a student at Eastern Michigan in Ypsilanti, majoring in French and then in Art. Our studies consumed many hours, so eight hours of sleep occurred only on Friday and Saturday nights. Our budget was slim, but we always tried to go out for dinner once a week, usually at some Italian restaurant or my favorite, The Old German in Ann Arbor. Football games in the Big House were a must, and we'd go to see an occasional movie.

We were blessed with our first child, Holly, who was born in Ann Arbor on December 8, 1960. Now there were three of us in our small, 8' x 35' trailer home. Sali became a full-time mom and we were learning to be parents.

By my junior year, life became more normal. I had a miniature dental practice at school which enabled me to complete my clinical requirements. It was made up of patients drawn out of the dental school pool of local people seeking inexpensive dental care. I did several gold inlays and a gold foil for Sali. It was exciting to think about graduating and starting a professional career.

A LUCKY C–

When we were juniors, we were assigned an operatory cubicle. This was our "dental office" for our junior and senior years. Here we performed all the operative dental procedures needed to fulfill our requirements for graduation. We selected patients from a waiting list and scheduled them for dental treatment. The procedures on our patients were broken down into successive steps. When we had completed a particular step, we put our name on a "ready list," which notified the clinical professors that we were ready for them to check our work.

By our junior year we had had courses from all of the dental professors and knew our favorites. This quite obviously influenced our clinical "ready list" signups. If we were sweating out completing a procedure and getting a good grade, it mattered a great deal as to which professor was coming into your cubicle to check your work. The professors on duty for any particular day would go to the list and take the next student's name. We never knew who was coming to check our work, but always hoped it was a professor we liked.

One of our professors was Dr. Sigurd Ramfjord. He was head of the Periodontics Department, which specialized in gingival (gum) and supporting (bone) tissue diseases. Dr. Ramfjord was noted for his research and high intelligence. As you might expect from his name, he was a Norwegian and had a significant Norwegian accent. We considered him to be a hard grader and none of us looked forward to having Dr. Ramfjord, or "Siggy," as we called him, stroll into our cubicle to check our work.

I was evidently destined to have the experience of having Dr. Ramfjord check my work that day. I had completed a particular procedure, had my patient ready to be examined, and had all my notes out ready to be checked. Dr. Ramfjord examined the work I had done on the patient, read my notes, reexamined my patient, and reread my notes. With a bit of a flourish, he spun around, looked at me, and said, in his thick Norwegian accent, "Yah Day; vell you did a gud job, I give you C–. I graciously replied, "Thank you, Dr. Ramfjord. Thank you very much!" Just another day in the life of a Michigan Dental student.

DENTAL SCRUBS & MICHIGAN'S FAMOUS DR. KAHN

One of our dental school requirements for graduation was to go over to the University hospital and scrub for a major surgery. A classmate, Ron Draheim, invited me to go along with him to get this requirement out of the way. He explained that his neighbor was a neurosurgery resident, and we could look him up on the surgical schedule and ask to scrub for his team. We went up to the surgical ward and found Ron's neighbor's name and the operating room he was working in. Also listed was the type of surgery they would be doing; "Tumor removal on the seventh cranial nerve." We found the operating room and were accepted as scrubs. Our first task was to go down the hall to where the surgical patients were being held, and ask the nurse to identify such and such a female patient. Then, we were to wrap her in an inflatable blanket, called a "Zoot-suit," and wheel her back to the surgery operatory. "No sweat," as we say in the Army. The nurse led us to a table, and lying there nude, and sedated was a red-headed woman about 45 years of age. Ron and I awkwardly looked at one another, and with no experience, and no instructions, we wrapped the patient in the plastic blanket and wheeled her back to the waiting surgical residents.

The surgical room was large and filled with various stainless-steel tables that had surgical instruments laid out on them. All the goodies the anesthesiologist used were there too, including TV monitors to show the patient's vital signs. Two or three large operatory lights hung above the patient. The two surgical residents, and two nurses, positioned the patient and hooked up the air to inflate the wrap Ron and I had put in place. The wrap was to help control blood pressure. The anesthesiologist began to monitor the patient's vital signs and control the depth of anesthesia. Several other surgical nurses were there getting all the surgical instruments in place. Now we began to wait for the head surgeon to arrive. Two surgical residents, one anesthesiologist, five surgical nurses, and two lowly dental students, all stood silently waiting for the head surgeon to arrive. This stretched out too long for the residents, so they decided to go ahead and start the surgery. The patient's head was shaved and then held firmly in position by screws in a metal halo device. One of the residents took a magic marker-like pen and sketched the incision lines. Working together, they made the incisions and reflected the thick cranial tissue back so the skull was visible. As this was happening, I was trying to keep from fainting! Then they took a trephine (a surgical drill), and began to remove cranial bone to get access to the brain.

BOOM!!! The door flew open. The head neurosurgeon had arrived—the beloved and famous, Dr. Edgar A. Kahn. I think everyone was trembling ... at least Ron and I were. Immediately, like a Field General, Doctor Kahn started giving commands and asking questions of the residents, of the anesthesiologist, and the nurses. "Turn the lights this way, no–that way. What's the patient's blood pressure; how old is this patient? What are we trying to accomplish here?" To the residents, "Describe exactly what you are doing and why?" Now his hands were right in there with the residents. We were all crowded in close as the procedure progressed. The brain on one side was exposed and the resident was told to carefully lift the brain to make it possible to view the tumor. My chin was practically on Dr. Kahn's shoulder as I tried to get a look at the tumor. Dr. Kahn spun around and said to me, "Tell me everything you know about tumors on the seventh cranial nerve." I replied, "Uh, uh, uh, I'm ah, I'm ah … ah dental student." He stared at me; the room was totally silent, and everyone was looking at me. Then Dr. Kahn said, "Don't they teach you anything about tumors on the seventh nerve in dental school?" I was speechless. He spun back around ,and they continued to remove the tumor. As quickly as he stormed in, he stormed out of the operating room. We could feel the pressure drop and a happier mood return as residents finished the operation. Dr. Kahn intrigued me, so I did a little research on him.

A MAGNIFICENT OBSESSION

Dr. Kahn was the son of a still famous architect, Albert Kahn, who designed many architecturally significant buildings in Detroit and on the Michigan campus in Ann Arbor. Most of them are still in use. Dr. Kahn finished his university and medical school and surgery residency, training in six years, instead of the normal nine or 10 years, and still found time to excel on the Michigan hockey team as its captain. He served in the U.S. Army in WWII as a surgeon, and was in the D-Day Invasion in Normandy, France. He was with the first group to enter Paris and his ability to speak six languages was a definite asset. Somewhere along the way Dr. Kahn obtained a pilot's license and flew around the Ann Arbor area with Charles Lindberg, who was, at that time, a test pilot for the Ford Motor Company at nearby Willow Run Airport. He was head of the Michigan Neurosurgery Department for 22 years and worked for a salary of $1.00 a year.

In 1929, when Dr. Kahn was 29 years old, Lloyd C. Douglas wrote the novel, *A MAGNIFICENT OBSESSION* which was eventually made into a blockbuster movie. The theme of the novel was taken from Matthew 6:1-4, which tells us to do good deeds for others in secret, and then God will reward you openly. Douglas served as a Congregational minister in Ann Arbor. It was not kept secret that Dr. Kahn was the surgeon who set the example that inspired Douglas to write the novel. Many professional honors were bestowed on Dr. Kahn. He set a very high bar to which any medical professional could aspire. Dr. Kahn inspires us all to use the gifts God has given us to bless others … and of course, in secret.

PART III

TIME TO MAKE
A LIVING

FINDING MY WAY

We graduated from dental school in May of 1962. I wanted to go to Alaska to practice dentistry and fulfill my childhood dream of hunting for big game. Also, I had been a student for six years, and I was anxious to earn a living in order to support my family and pay off my educational debts. Moving to Alaska seemed like a good choice to me, but in hindsight ... I may have been asking too much of Sali and Beatrice, my mother-in-law. They were good troopers, and did not object.

I borrowed money from my dad in order to fly up to Fairbanks and take the Alaska State Dental Board. I couldn't practice dentistry in Alaska without passing their Board. At that time, there were certain desirable states like Alaska, Hawaii, Arizona, New Mexico, Florida, California, and Colorado that made their Dental Boards almost impossible to pass. The old "Bucks" that were well established and making big incomes did not want a flood of young dentists infringing on their turf. There was the possibility that I might not pass the Board, which never entered my mind; so ... off I went, full of "Go Blue!" optimism.

I stayed the night in the famous Nordale Hotel in downtown Fairbanks. My second floor room had a south-facing window which in July meant the sun shone in all night. It was so hot that I had to sleep with the window open. Several drunks spent the whole night below my window—talking, laughing, and swigging on a bottle of cheap booze. Hence, very little sleep for me.

Tired, but loaded with adrenalin, I aroused myself the next morning for my big day! It was amazing to me that, eight years after my discharge from the Army, I took the Board at the hospital on Ladd Field, now Fort Wainwright, within eyesight of my old Army hut. Memories of sleeping out at 63 degrees below zero, a possible court martial, basketball games, and names of Army buddies, flooded my mind.

For the next two days I sweated out all the tasks we had to perform. It was a great relief when I was informed that I had passed the Board.

Now I was qualified to practice dentistry in Alaska. If I had failed the Board, our lives would have been very different.

DR. BILL SEIG

During my senior year in dental school, I had searched through the American Dental Association Directory looking for Michigan Dental graduates practicing in Alaska. I found five of them, and wrote each a letter expressing my interest in practicing dentistry in Alaska. Three of them replied. One was Dr. Bill Seig who had previously practiced in Battle Creek, Michigan. He was now practicing in the small town of Haines, Alaska, which is at the northern end of the Inside Passage. He was very encouraging in his reply to my letter. I had no idea, nor did he mention, that he was on the Dental Board and would be one of my examiners! This was obviously to my advantage.

After the Board exam, he invited me to drive with him down the ALCAN Highway to his home in Haines. We piled into his little Volkswagen Bug and took off for a two-day drive to Haines. Dr. Bill loved Alaska and told me many stories about his life there. He encouraged me to check out the dental practices for sale in Juneau and Petersburg. He said, "You don't want to live up in Fairbanks where it's 50 degrees below zero in the winter."

I spent two special days in Haines with Dr. Bill and his lovely wife. Then I boarded my first ride in a twin-engine, amphibious Grumman Goose. These eight-passenger planes were the backbone of travel in Southeast Alaska where most island communities had no runway. The only way to get to Petersburg was by flight in a Goose. I went and checked out both the Juneau and Petersburg dental practices

The day I flew down to Petersburg was a beautiful day … sunshine and blue sky, with magnificent snow-capped mountains the whole way. I was absolutely captured by the scenery and beauty of Southeast Alaska, and I decided to buy the Petersburg practice. Little did I know that I was seeing the exception to an area that was, most of the time, cloudy with drizzling rain. I mean, you could go 30 days and not see the sun shine. It takes many days for 110 inches, (average yearly rainfall in Petersburg), to drizzle down out of the heavens.

I flew back to Ann Arbor, to Sali and little Holly. A couple days later, I somehow decided to look through the want ads in the Detroit newspaper. Again, God would provide. Miracle of miracles, there in the Detroit paper was an ad looking for someone to drive a new Chevy pickup truck to a man in Fairbanks, Alaska. I called, was interviewed, approved, and now we had transportation to Alaska.

ALASKA BOUND

In August of 1962, we said goodbye to my family in Detroit. After that, Sali and I packed all our worldly goods into 16 boxes and loaded them into the truck. With 18-month-old Holly between us, we headed for Grand Rapids to say good-bye to Mom Spoor, Sali's sister Judy and her husband Elden, and our special friends. The last goodbye was to our dear friends Jack and Anne Rudell. Jack gave us a tour of his new dental office, after which we said our last, few parting words. As we drove away into the setting sun, I looked in the rear view mirror and could see Jack, my best friend in life, standing there alone and waving. Sali and I were crying. Little Holly was standing on the seat between us. I had the strongest urge to turn around and stay there with Jack. It was, perhaps, the better choice, but my nature is not to change course, so I just kept driving on, another pivotal life decision.

We drove to Ludington and put the truck on the Lake Michigan car ferry named "Badger" for the voyage across the lake to Manitowoc, Wisconsin. I planned to camp out every night and fish many streams all the way to Haines, so I had a tarp, sleeping bags, a camp stove, fly rod, etc., all packed in the truck. After we debarked from the Badger in the morning, we drove all day, and rolled into a campground in western Wisconsin well after dark. Everyone but us had already settled in for the night. All the parking spots were taken, but I finally found a place in which to squeeze the truck and set up our camp—a tarp fastened to the side of the truck. We slid into our double sleeping bag, with Holly between us, and quickly fell asleep. The next morning, we peered out from under the tarp opening to a continual parade of legs passing by. We discovered that in the dark, I had camped right on the trail to the biffy. The whole camp ground was marching past our tarp on the way to the John. How embarrassing.

By the following evening, we were in South Dakota. I located a pullout next to a beautiful clear stream, which brought visions of trout for dinner. As soon as we were about to set up camp, a car full of noisy teenage boys from a nearby Indian reservation pulled up. They had plans to drink beer and have a bond fire. This did not sit well with Sali or me, so we pulled up stakes and headed for the nearest motel. That was the end of our campouts and my fishing hopes. From then on, it was motel city every night … except for a stop in Pocatello, Idaho. We stopped to visit an army buddy of mine and his family. They were strong Mormons. I remember his wife saying, after we had been there a couple days, "You know, we only have Mormon friends, but gee, you're just like us." We all laughed.

After nine days and a 1000 miles of gravel road on the ALCAN Highway, I dropped Sali and Holly off at Dr Seig's home in Haines, Alaska. Then, I drove on up the ALCAN to deliver the truck to its new owner in Fairbanks.

A day later, Dr. Bill put Sali and Holly on a Grumman Goose bound for Juneau. They experienced the same beautiful blue sky and sunshine, snowcapped mountains with mountain goats and glaciers, that I had seen on my first flight to Juneau and Petersburg. Unfortunately, they had to spend a night in the old, damp, and moldy Juneau Hotel. They had a new Alaskan experience of having to share a common bathroom with the whole floor—all men.

The next day, I flew down from Fairbanks to Juneau to meet them. We then flew to Petersburg in another Goose. We were unexpectedly blessed to have many boxes of our material possessions—that we had mailed back in Great Falls, Montana, arrive with us on our flight.

LITTLE NORWAY

Petersburg, sometimes called "Little Norway," was a Norwegian fishing community of 1600 people on Mitkof Island in Southeast Alaska. This island was one of the hundreds of islands that make up the Alexander Archipelago, lying off the coast of southeast Alaska. It is 10 miles wide and 17 miles long. Before the fishermen and loggers moved in, it was inhabited by the Tlingit (cling kit) Indians, many of whom still live there.

The archipelago contains all of the Tongass National Forest—a vast rainforest of Hemlock and Spruce trees. Logging, commercial fishing for salmon, halibut, and crab, are the primary means of making a living in Petersburg. This area of Alaska is a Sportsman's Paradise with fishing for salmon, Cutthroat and Steelhead trout. There is also Brown bear and Black bear, Mountain goat, and Sitka Black-tailed deer hunting. In the fall, geese and ducks arrive by the thousands.

Petersburg, Alaska.

The first home we rented was a tiny Norwegian style house supported by pilings driven into the soggy muskeg. In general the term "muskeg" describes what I would call an ancient bog that is primarily composed of decaying organic matter. The ground cover contains moss, lichens, berry bushes, and in the drier areas—gnarly, stunted, black spruce trees struggling to survive. The muskeg terrain is a sort of gelatinous, moss-covered mass, pocked with deep, dangerous, water ponds called "muskeg holes." When Sali did the laundry, the house rocked back and forth to the rhythm of the washing machine.

Our water supply was from a lake formed by damming up a stream

Holly, Sali, and Heather meeting Alaska Air PBY.

high in the muskeg. The resulting water was the color of weak tea with lots of organic matter and little red worms wiggling in it. They were alive in cold water and dead in hot water. Climbing into a bathtub of hot tea colored water with dead little red worms floating in it was definitely a new experience. Sali felt like she was on another planet.

Also, we discovered little bugs floating in our breakfast cereal. Sali thought that everyone must have them. Weeks later we found out that this was not so. It took Sali several weeks of hard work to get rid of them. Ugh! Apparently, they were passed on to us by the previous renter.

We Michiganders had to learn a whole new vocabulary of words used by fishermen, loggers, and our Norwegian neighbors. I remember a handy little Norwegian word, "Uff da!" that covered several expressions like, "oops," or "Oh no."

Holly and Heather in the Petersburg Fourth of July parade.

So, there we were, Dick, Sali, and little Holly; 3000 miles from home and family and didn't know a soul … $13,000 in debt to my dad for the dental practice … $3000 owed to my mother-in-law … and $5000 owed to the University of Michigan. We did, however, have an Alaskan dental license and had rented the small dental office of the previous dentist. Now we were hoping that someone might call for a dental appointment so I could generate some badly needed income. "Oh Lord, please let the phone ring." Well, actually, we had no phone, no television, no radio, and not even a record player. "Please knock … Someone! Anyone!"

Petersburg fishing boats.

The boat I built in Petersburg.

STRANGE BEGINNINGS

The first week we were there, I opened my dental practice in the small cottage office. At the same time, I came down with Montezuma's Revenge, or "back door trots," and I was unable to work. It's typical for newcomers to Petersburg to contract "Montezuma's Revenge" from bacteria in the muskeg water. I was home in bed, when a nighttime knock came to our entryway door. Sali answered the knock. There, in our entry, stood a tall Tlingit Indian with a very swollen face. He was in urgent need of a dentist. My terrified wife called me down from the bedroom. In my miserable condition, I appeared in my pajamas and told the young man to see me in the morning. Then I went back to bed.

A few minutes later … there was another knock at the door. Sali was not about to answer it, so she called me down again. I figured it was the same guy, so I pulled the door open. There stood two rather prominent women of Petersburg wanting to introduce themselves to the new dental family—a terrified wife, a 20-month-old daughter, and a diarrhetic, financially broke, dentist in his pajamas. This was not a very impressive beginning for the new dentist in town. Our welcoming committee was composed of Ethel Bergmann, the local school principal's wife, and Ruth Sandvik, a grade school teacher and librarian. After introductions and explanations, we all had a good laugh and thus began lifelong friendships. Somehow the conversation led to the fact that I had made $11.00 that week. By the end of the evening, Ruth had written out a check to me for dental care that I had yet to provide for her.

God often provides in strange and unusual ways. It's important to take time in your life to look back and see how God always provides, "And my God shall supply all your need according to His riches in glory by Christ Jesus" (Philippians 4:19). This is a comforting confidence builder if there ever was one. A good Scripture to commit to memory.

MY FIRST MOOSE HUNT

In September 1962, just after we had moved to Petersburg, Dr. Seig invited me to go moose hunting with him in the Haines area. On the flight to Haines, I stopped in Juneau to purchase a rifle. My Winchester lever action Model 94 was not adequate for moose hunting. I found a nice sporting goods store in the downtown area. One of the clerks showed me several rifles that would fit my needs. I chose a Remington 7mm because I thought it was a rifle that could last me for years and be all that I needed for my Alaskan hunting. There was also a "Buck" knife there that I couldn't pass up. Now I was all set to begin the many years of big game hunting that I had dreamed of doing when I was a 15-year-old ninth grader in Memphis, Tennessee.

Then I caught the next Grumman Goose flight to Haines where Bill Seig met me. He introduced me to the other guys who were going to hunt with us; his neighbor, Marty Cordes, and a friend, Forest Young. I was, by far, the kid in the group and the least experienced hunter.

At dinner, Bill told me the story of a moose hunt Forest and Marty had gone on seven years earlier. They had driven 30 miles north of Haines to their cabin on Chilkoot Lake. From there they went up the Chilkoot River another 15 miles in a motorized canoe. They shot two moose a couple miles above their camp. They loaded up the canoe, and Marty took several loads of meat back to Haines. On their final day Marty went grouse hunting and Forest headed to their kill area to bring back a moose hide. When Forest got to the kill area the bears had taken over. Forest had many years of hunting experience in bear country and knew that most bears ran off when confronted by a man. With this in mind he took only his pack board to retrieve the moose hide he had hung in a tree. As he was lowering the moose hide, he saw two Brown bears in the distance. He yelled and waved his arms to drive them off. One bear took off, but the other charged him and pulled him down as he tried to climb the tree. The bear chewed him up badly and treated him like a rag doll! He finally dropped him, bleeding and severely wounded. Forest decided to play dead, but his mouth began to fill with blood and saliva so he had to roll over in order to breathe. The bear was immediately upon him again and took a few more bites before leaving.

Marty, seeing that Forest was late for their rendezvous time, hiked to the kill area and found Forest in very bad shape. He provided what first aid he could, hiked back two miles to camp, brought back a sleeping bag, food, shotgun, and a Coleman lantern. He then slid Forest into the sleeping bag, laid the shotgun next to him, lit the lantern, and headed back to Haines in the canoe. It was about three in the afternoon.

By the time Marty had gone to Haines, 15 miles by river and 30 miles by highway, got a rescue party, and came back up the river in the dark, 13 hours had passed. As they carried Forest on a stretcher to their camp, they could hear the bear following in the brush behind them. At first light, a Canadian Royal Air Force helicopter flew in from White Horse, Yukon Territory, and took Forest to Haines, from there an amphibious PBY (a large, amphibious, twin-engine aircraft, developed for use in WWII. There are a number of them that have been restored by private owners) took him to a hospital in Juneau. It's a much longer story found in a book by Ben East entitled *Great Escapes*. You can buy it on Amazon. Yes, Forest miraculously survived.

The next morning, our hunting party assembled at Marty's house and took off for Chilkoot Lake. I was in for a surprise, since no one had told me we would be using an airboat for the hunt. Bill handed me a heavy insulated coverall, a wool beanie, a pair of heavy gloves, and a pair of aviator goggles. I gave him a dumb look, and he said, "Put 'em on!"

The airboat had an airplane engine mounted high above and near the stern of the flat bottom boat. The driver's seat was in front of the grilled-in prop and above a three-passenger seat. Forest climbed up into the driver's seat and the rest of us piled into the passenger seat. Forest cranked up the Lycoming aircraft engine, and we were going 30 miles an hour in a minute. It was like we were flying along in an open cockpit biplane. Since we were sitting right in front of the prop, the rush of air over us made for a very chilly ride. I then understood all the clothing.

We headed up and out of the lake into the Chilkoot River, and towards the Canadian border some 90 miles away. It was a beautiful fall day. There had already been a couple hard frosts and the birch trees were all dressed in yellow. There was some new snow on the distant mountains above the 4000 foot level making a beautiful picture against the cloudless blue sky. We stopped and checked out favorable areas the Haines boys had hunted before. Each time we stopped we had to remove all our warm clothing in order to comfortably hunt on foot. We covered a lot of territory in the airboat, but saw no moose. By evening we had returned to our starting launch site on Chilkoot Lake. It had been a beautiful day, and a beautiful hunt, but no meat for the freezer.

The next day we again hunted the braids of the Chilkat River, but closer to Haines. We paired up, Bill and Forest hunted together and Marty and I hunted together. The river was shallow enough in the areas we were hunting so we could just wear hip boots. It was a long day of walking and wading. Late in the afternoon, Marty spotted a young bull. I was the guest, so he offered me the first shot. My new 7mm had open sights but no scope. I had sighted it in before our hunt in a gravel pit near Haines and felt comfortable with taking the shot. The only challenge was to take a standing shot from our location out in the river. I brought my rifle up to sight on my target. Marty yells, "Hurry and take your shot!" The moose was about to go behind a long row of spruce trees and I would not be able to get a shot. The young bull was ambling along in three feet of water about 75 yards away from me. I tried to hold on his shoulder and squeezed off a shot. POW! A second shot and I had my first bull moose.

Bill and Forest had heard my shot and headed our way. After some discussion relating to a dislike for having to gut out the moose in three feet of water, the four of us tried, but couldn't drag the moose up a two-foot bank so that we could do the butchering on dry land. No such luck, the bull was too heavy, even for the four of us, to pull up the bank. So, we had to butcher him in two feet of water. We went home that night satisfied with our success and meat for the table. I flew back to Petersburg with our first Alaska moose meat. For reasons I cannot explain … Bill and I never hunted together again. It saddens me to think back on this missed opportunity. How could I not pursue this friendship with my mentor and "Michigan Man," Bill Seig? He died as a rather young man in his early 60s, before he could enjoy his retirement.

A MISSIONARY ADVENTURE

While living in Petersburg, we attended Saint Andrew's Episcopal Church. Our priest was Henry Chapman. Henry's father, John Chapman, was the first Episcopal missionary assigned to the small lower Yukon Athabascan village of Anvik. He founded the Christ Church Mission there in 1887. Henry was the first white child to be born in Anvik in 1895. When his father retired in 1930, Henry became the Episcopal priest in Anvik. He was assigned to Saint Andrews church in Petersburg in 1960. This was going to be his retiring parish.

Father Chapman, as we called him, asked me to serve on the church vestry and I gladly accepted. This caused me to go to the annual Alaska Episcopal Convocation held in Juneau. There I met Father Chapman's successor, Father Dick Mc Ginnis.

In conversation with Father McGinnis, he related to me that a dentist had never been to Anvik, a village of about 90 people. He said that the people there had dire dental needs. This led to my offering to fly up to Anvik and provide dental care for the children and emergency care, such as extractions, for the adults.

I contacted the Bethel Public Health dentist, Dr. Richard Mittlestadt. Bethel, at the time, was a large (2000+) Native community on the Kuskokwim River 140 miles south of Anvik. I explained to Dr. Mittlestadt my desire to provide dental care to the village of Anvik and asked him if he could help me get the portable dental equipment I needed. He was more than willing to loan me whatever he had in his inventory. Then he referred me to a local bush pilot for the flight to Anvik.

On Sunday, November 17, 1963, I flew from Petersburg to Anchorage, spent the night, and the next day flew on to Bethel where I was a guest of the Mittlestadt's. The following day was spent selecting and loading the dental equipment into a Cessna 185 on skis. The pilot added several bundles of mail to the load as well. I remember taking off for Anvik about mid-afternoon.

I was an excited passenger looking down hoping to spot a moose or a wolf out on the tundra, but they were well hidden that day. We headed north to land on the frozen Yukon River at the small village of Holy Cross. A number of villagers, including adults and children, came out to meet the plane. In remote Alaskan communities, the arrival of the mail plane is a village event. The pilot delivered the bundle of mail and then we continued on to Anvik.

Sunset in late November in this part of Alaska is about 4:30 pm. We landed in Anvik in the evening twilight and taxied our ski plane up to the village. A number of people came out to greet us. This group was led by two young women who ran up to my door as I exited the plane.

They excitedly greeted me, "Oh, Dr. Day! Oh, Dr. Day! We are the village health aides. We will be delivering a "breech baby" tonight. We need you to help us."

I didn't know what to say. I wanted to hop back into the plane and tell the pilot to take off! Recovering from the shock, I said, "Ah, er, ah, well … they didn't teach us to deliver babies in dental school, but, but, … I can boil water. Well … if you really need me, come to the McGinnis' cabin and wake me up."

I told Father McGinnis the story. He got a great laugh over my "delivery" dilemma, and said he thought that everything will work out OK. Words of a man of great Faith.

Before retiring that night, I went to the school library where I would be seeing my dental patients. I set up my equipment for tomorrow's effort. Sleep did not come, I lay awake all night fearing a knock on my door.

The next morning at breakfast, the health aides dropped by … all joyful and laughing. They had delivered a healthy baby without a problem. I wanted to say: "That's really great. But you owe me a night's sleep." Thankfully, for the next 48 years of my career, I was never again called upon to deliver a baby.

After breakfast I headed for the library to begin seeing my patients, mostly grade school children. The school had arranged for the teachers to send the children to me in pairs. I entered my library operatory to find that all my hand instruments were frozen in a block of my sterilizing solution, Zephiran Chloride. No one had told me that the library wasn't heated during the night. I took my frozen block of instruments to the Mc Ginnis' kitchen and spent an hour thawing them out. This delayed my seeing patients, but no harm.

I worked from Wednesday through most of Friday seeing almost all of the grade school children. For children who had never been to a dentist before, they were excellent patients. They sat quietly, whispering to each other, waiting their turn. I tried to enter into a conversation with several of the children, but even with the offer of two dollars, I had no success. Other than fillings and extractions on the children, I also removed a few adult teeth. All in all, I felt my missionary effort was worthwhile. The community was very appreciative. They had a special dinner for me and presented me with two beautiful woven grass baskets.

On the last day I worked, Friday, November 22, 1963, President Kennedy was assassinated in Dallas, Texas. The news traveled fast ... even to little Anvik by that afternoon.

Father McGinnis decided to have a memorial service that evening. The temperature was near zero. Father McGinnis built a fire in the wood stove in the small, beautiful chapel lit mostly by candle light. About 20 of us adults slowly gathered in the pews for the service to begin.

I clearly remember kneeling for the prayers. My feet were freezing and my forehead was sweating. Here I was honoring our deceased President in prayer with a small group of Athabascan Natives far, far away from the Lower 48 States. The prayers from the Episcopal or more properly Anglican, Book of Common Prayer were beautiful. I was brought to tears listening to my Native brothers and sisters in Christ recite the prayers.

As we recited the prayers I knew we were coming to the word, "propitiation." "It's a beautiful word, found only three times in the King James Bible. We seldom use it in our daily conversation and certainly not in the Athabascan language. Its definition was not clearly understood by me at the time of this service. I wondered how my assembled communicants would pronounce it. The prayer went smoothly without a pause for the pronunciation of propitiation.

My hope was that Father McGinnis had clearly explained to his congregants the meaning of propitiation so that they knew it meant Christ's sacrificial death was an appeasement, a turning away, of the wrath of God due us for our sins and, thus, a means of our being reconciled to God.

After the service, we all walked quietly out into the ambient light of the still Alaskan night. A small group of Episcopal Believers, far, far, away from the heart of America, had paid their honor to our deceased President. Tomorrow I will be on my way back home to be with my family for our Thanksgiving celebration in Petersburg.

Holy Cross children greet us as we land on the frozen Yukon River.

Food and storage cache.

THE LEMON DROP KID

After we had lived in Petersburg a couple years, I joined the Rotary Club and attended their weekly luncheon meetings. A letter arrived addressed to the president of our club. A certain Ron Hall had passed through Petersburg on the ferry, and he was in awe of the beauty of the distant mainland mountains. He wondered if there was anyone he could hire to take him hiking in the beautiful mountains he had seen from the ferry. Our club president handed me the letter and asked if I would answer it. This led to my writing a letter inviting Mr. Hall to come to Petersburg and I offered to take him on a hike in the mountains he had admired.

On an early August afternoon, the ferry boat with Ron Hall arrived—all 5 feet 4 inches of him.

I had given him a list of things he needed for the hike. The one item he still needed was boots that fit. His shoe size and budgetary restrictions led us to the children's department of Petersburg's only variety store. The kids in Petersburg frequently wore what were called "Breakup Boots." They were black rubber with a wide red band around the top. The kids wore them during "Spring Break Up" when all the ice and snow was melting. These were the only boots available in Ron's size.

The next day, we loaded our gear into my 20-foot river boat that I had built, and headed for the entrance to Le Conte Glacier Bay. It was a seven-mile trip across Frederick Sound to the shores of Horn Cliffs, and then a few more miles down to the bay entrance. We motored up into a stream that flowed into the bay near its mouth. It was a warm sunny day, and the tide was high enough to allow me to motor upstream and anchor the boat. Ron was very excited about this adventure! It was far removed from his vocation as an organist at a Los Angeles Christian Science Church which was where Doris Day, the famous actress and singer, attended. You know, my famous actress/singer cousin? Ha!

I had hunted this area of Horn Cliffs for goats the previous October, and I thought it would be an easy climb for Ron. I planned to camp out one night and return the next day. Our backpacks contained a light sleeping bag, rain coat, Primus stove, small tarp, cooking pot, and food for two meals and, of course, I had my trusty 7mm rifle.

After securing the boat, we headed in the direction I felt to be the easiest way to reach an area that was a good place to spend the night. The climb took us to an elevation of 1000 feet. Our progress was going well, but it was so warm that we had to stop first to remove a jacket, then a shirt, and finally we were down to our tee-shirts and still sweating. Ron brought along a big bag of his favorite trail treats—lemon drops. He called out to me about every 15 minutes, "Hey Dick, how about a lemon drop?"

We were about a half hour into our hike, when I noticed a big pile of fresh bear scat. I casually pointed this out to Ron and kept on moving. Soon another pile of bear scat appeared, and again I pointed this out to Ron. From then on, I noticed the lemon drop stops were more frequent, and "The Lemon Drop Kid" followed just three or four steps behind me. The climb was going well, the walking was easy, so I felt I had chosen a good way to the top. After about three hours of climbing, we reached the end of the valley and were looking at vertical rock walls. Try as I might, I couldn't find a trail or chute to lead us up any further. The end result was to spend the night here and hike back out tomorrow.

We found a good spot in the tall Spruce trees to camp, laid out our tarps, and gathered wood for a fire. I announced to Ron that I needed to go down to the stream for water, maybe 40 yards away. Ron quickly said, "I'll go along." I said, "Okay, whatever suits you." I grabbed my water pot and headed for the stream with Ron at my heels. A freeze-dried spaghetti dinner was on the menu. Then for a treat, I decided to heat up some dried apricots with water from the stream as well. I always brought these along on hunting and fishing trips. It was like I had served Ron flaming Cherries Jubilee. He raved and raved about this desert. He said he had never had anything like it. The rest of the evening was spent tending our fire and chatting.

That night, Ron told me he had expected I would be taking him on well-established trails—trails with steps and railings, similar to the ones he climbed in California. He admitted that the bear scat caused him to fear for his safety and made him pray wrongfully. I'm not sure how Christian Scientists pray, but fear of a bear did not produce proper prayers. This bothered Ron a great deal and he must have needed to confess to me to assuage his guilt. By midnight, I was talked out and crawled into my sleeping bag. Somewhere around 2 or 3 a.m. I awoke to see Ron still wide awake and feeding the fire. Without any comment, I rolled over to sleep some more. By 6 a.m. I was up and making breakfast. Ron had spent the whole night tending the fire out of fear that a bear might attack us. There was nothing I could say that might comfort him. We packed up and headed back to the boat in a light drizzle—Ron following practically in my back pocket.

When we reached the boat, we discovered the tide was out, and our craft was perched on a few large rocks in the stream. This seemed to distress Ron a great deal; our trip home was threatened and possibly cancelled till the tide came in and floated the boat. With bears in the area, he wanted to get away as soon as possible. I sized up our situation and began to unload the boat of everything not screwed down; the motor, gas cans, anchor, etc. Ron stood on the bank watching. Once I had lightened the boat as much as possible, I took an oar to use as a pry bar and levered the boat off the rocks and out into the middle of the stream. There was only about six inches of water, but this was enough to allow me to maneuver the boat downstream about 100 yards to deeper water. Ron saw what I was accomplishing and with great excitement. He ran along the bank dancing and shouting like Rumple Stiltskin; "Oh, this is a miracle. Oh, I have never seen anything like this. Oh, you're a genius." I had a happy client. We loaded up the boat and headed home. Wet, cold, and tired, we motored into the Petersburg channel. I blew my air horn as we passed our house to let Sali know we'd soon be home. Nothing like a hot meal, a hot shower and a warm bed.

Because of our experience at Horn Cliffs, I thought Ron was sure to hop on the next ferry to Juneau and return to California. However, this was not to be. My father was visiting us, and we had plans to go salmon fishing the next day. Dad and I had decided to go up into Thomas Bay and fish for Coho Salmon. There is a large glacial field along the Canadian—Alaskan border and one of the glaciers extends west to terminate at the head of Thomas Bay. Ron wanted to go along with us to take pictures of this area. Fortunately, I did not tell him a certain story in a book written by a Petersburg resident, Virginia Culp. It was about the "Little Green Men" who lived in Thomas Bay.

Sali made sack lunches for us and I loaned Ron my new 35mm camera since his camera was not adequate to take good photos. The day was typical Southeast Alaska—overcast and drizzly as we headed north east across Frederick Sound into the mouth of Thomas Bay.

Ron wanted to hike up the tidal flats that led to the glacier's face, so we dropped him off and told him that we would be back in an hour. Carrying his sack lunch with my camera hanging around his neck, and wearing his new break-up boots, he disappeared in the direction of the receding glacier. Dad and I headed for a few spots where we felt the salmon should be schooled up. Our fishing produced only a few beat-up Pink Salmon, which we threw back. It was soon time to pick up Ron and return home.

In coastal Alaska all the fishermen pay close attention to the tides, which change every six hours. I did not accurately pay close attention to the stage of the tide when we dropped Ron off, but I knew it was near low tide, which gave Ron at least an hour to hike around. We arrived at the spot where we had dropped Ron off, and he was not in sight. It was apparent that the tide had changed, and was now coming in. I stood on the deck of my boat and glassed toward the glacier hoping to spot our wayward photographer. We let the boat slowly float in with the rising water. Fortunately, within five or 10 minutes I spotted a distant head pop up then disappear, then reappear in a different spot. It was up, down, up, down, appear, disappear, and reappear, as Ron made his way toward us. A terrified, strung out, Ron arrived at the boat! His story was that he had smooth going toward the glacier until he noticed that the tide was coming in, and the puddles he had to cross were going from ankle-deep to knee-deep. Fortunately, he turned around to retrace his steps and head back. As the tide came in, he had to wade across deeper and deeper pools. Soon, he was up to his waist—and just before he reached us, the water was up to his armpits. By then panic had set in. He caught sight of me standing up in the boat and forged ahead. Thankfully he reached us just in time, hypothermia wasn't far away. We hauled him into the boat. While he related his traumatic story, I noticed that he was soaked almost to his shoulders. Oddly enough his paper bag lunch was dry as a bone and my expensive camera was still hanging around his neck … with salt water dripping out of it. He apologized for not holding it over his head. Needless to say, I was glad to have Ron back in the boat—scared spitless, cold and wet, but ALIVE. That was the absolute end of my volunteer guide business. Didn't I learn back in the Army … never raise your hand, never volunteer for anything. Apparently not.

WHAT SHALL WE DO

Our second daughter, Heather, was born in our small Petersburg hospital on February 12, 1964. For Holly's birth in Ann Arbor, Michigan, I was not allowed in the delivery room. At the Petersburg hospital however, they welcomed me in. The attending physician was Dr. Smith. He had practiced in Wisconsin, but his love for bear hunting drew him to Petersburg. The room was windowless and rather warm. I was wearing my favorite wool Pendleton shirt as I stood watching Sali give birth. I started to faint … and quickly a couple nurses held me up as they guided me to a seat. There I watched Heather's birth from a distance. So now we were a family of four. We were happy with God's blessing of two precious daughters.

By the fall of 1966, our time in Petersburg was coming to an end. I had enjoyed starting a small town dental practice from scratch, but we both missed our family, friends, and sunshine in Michigan. I enjoyed all the aspects of dentistry. However, I was frustrated to see so many children with orthodontic problems that I could not solve. The closest orthodontist was in Seattle, 800 miles away and of no practical help.

I wrote Dr. Robert Aldrich, a Professor of Orthodontics at the University of Michigan Dental School, and one of my favorite instructors. I described to him the orthodontic problems I was seeing in my young patients and my frustration with being unable to treat them. He graciously replied with some treatment suggestions, but my basic training from dental school was not enough for me to tackle the comprehensive orthodontic problems of my patients.

Sali and I discussed my desire to go back to Ann Arbor to get a graduate degree in orthodontics. I decided that I should apply to Rackham Graduate School for entrance into Michigan's Orthodontic Program. If I had known how slim the odds of my getting in were, I doubt that I would have even applied. We later found out that there were 180 applicants for a class of eight. I filled out the forms, and with minimal optimism, sent them to Rackham. By now, Heather was two and Holly was five. We couldn't envision spending the rest of our lives in Petersburg, so far away from our families. Going back to Ann Arbor gave us two years to be with our families and friends before returning to Alaska. Only this time … we were Anchorage-bound!

AN EAGLE CREEK RAM

My Petersburg friend, Gordon Edgars, an experienced sheep hunter, had already taken nine Dall sheep rams from Alaska's Wrangell Mountains. He did this in nine successive years. This is an unheard-of accomplishment for a sheep hunter today. Gordy invited me to go on a sheep hunt in the Wrangells with him and two of his U.S. Forest Service friends. We flew up to Cordova in mid-August, 1966 and stayed at the famous old hotel—The Windsor. It was an historical remnant of the copper mining era in the early 1920's. Sadly, it burned down the year after we were there.

In 1911, the first train loads of extremely high-grade copper ore from the Kennicott mine arrived in Cordova. It was then loaded aboard ships bound for Seattle. The rail line of 196 miles was built under very difficult conditions along the Copper River between 1908 and 1911. There is a book by Rex Beach, titled *The Iron Trail*, telling the story about the two companies that competed to be the first to build the rail line from the Kennicott mine to Cordova. Another famous author, Jack London, spent some time in Cordova, also writing novels about Alaska. Sidney Lawrence, Alaska's famous Gold Rush artist, spent time as well, painting in Cordova. I doubt that we could purchase one of his paintings today for less than $50,000. They are rarely for sale. Museums, corporations, and wealthy people own most of them.

The next day, our sheep hunting party hired a famous "bush" pilot, Mud Hole Smith, to fly us north to May Creek. The landing strip was at least 5000 feet long and had been used to bring in a small herd of buffalo around 1948. The herd has grown and is still in the area. We were met at the air strip by an old-timer, Walter Holmes, a friend of Gordy's. He took us to his house where we spent the night.

Walter and his wife, Tess, lived out in the middle of nowhere; in what is now part of the Wrangell-Saint Elias National Park. They were both in their seventies. After a delicious spaghetti dinner that Tess made for us, I wandered through several sheds near Walter's house. They were mostly filled with old mining equipment. Then I noticed an old bulldozer made by the Diebold Safe and Lock Company. This company still exists today! Further poking around revealed two old Chrysler cars from the 1920s, in very good shape. Some years later, a car collector discovered them, bought them from Walter, and flew them out to be restored.

As a young man, Walter transported mining parts and mail by dog team from Kulane Lake, in the Yukon Territory, up over the Skolai Pass, then down to McCarthy for delivery to the Kennicott Copper Mine. Get a map and trace this route out, and you will see how difficult a task this must have been. Kulane Lake is on the ALCAN Highway northwest of White Horse, Yukon Territory. Bill Seig and I stayed in a lodge on the lake when we drove from Fairbanks to Haines, after I had taken the Dental Board.

The next morning Walter loaded us and our gear into his old WWII military truck. He drove us six miles to the Dan Creek mine, where we would begin our arduous climb to our hunting cabin.

I had never seen the remnants of a large, old placer mine, which dated back to the early 1900s. Placer mines are located along stream and river beds. The gold bearing sand and gravel is washed in a series of screens or sluices to retrieve the gold. The Dan Creek Mine was one of the richest placer mines in Alaska. It yielded about 70,000 ounces of gold. The price of gold today, April 9, 2024, as I edit my editor's edit, is $2390 per ounce. That makes 70,000 ounces worth $167,300,000. There's still gold there … let's go!

Most of the mine buildings were intact but in bad shape and slowly falling down. We explored all the buildings that were safe enough to go through—mess hall, office, bunk house, stable, and a large machine shop. As I walked through those old, silent, decaying structures, I could hear the echoes and voices of horses and men who worked the mine so many years ago. Now it was abandoned … quiet, decaying, and returning to the earth … like we all eventually do. Our tour gave me a very melancholy feeling. A paraphrase from *The Message* in James 4:14, "What is the nature of our life? We are but a wisp of vapor, a puff of smoke, that is visible for a moment … then vanishes."

The four of us started out with heavy backpacks close to 60 pounds, plus our rifles. Our trail led upstream on the bed rock of Dan Creek. We hadn't gone a hundred yards, when Dean Weeden suddenly shouted, "I found a gold nugget!" Sure enough, he had spotted a dime-sized nugget in a small pool in the bedrock. How lucky can you get? It's the only nugget our hunting party found. Within a half-mile, we came to a place where a long rope hung down from a tree 40 feet up a vertical bank. A couple of us had to climb up to the tree base, haul up our packs and rifles, then help pull the last two guys up.

The trail continued up the mountain side. It was overgrown with thick alders in many parts. Years ago, horses were used to haul mining equipment and supplies to the upper reaches of the creek, and to bring mined gold and minerals out. The trail that once accommodated horses and wagons was now only a narrow foot trail. A huge mountain rock slide had obliterated a long stretch of the trail, making it dicey to traverse with a heavy backpack—one slip, and you fell down the rock slide to the creek bottom, at least 1000 feet below.

We spent five hours going only five miles up the trail reaching an altitude of about 4000 feet. It was a clear, sunny, August day. The scenery was awesome. I wondered how many miners and horses had followed this same trail some 40 years earlier. We were now about an hour from our destination—an old log cabin that the early gold miners had built.

Five hours up a difficult trail left us all sweaty and tired. Now we were faced with two choices: to climb up a steep hill between us and the cabin, or try to ford the glacier fed creek—a narrow, freezing torrent of snow melt. We decided to try to ford the stream by making a human chain. The first and heaviest guy was to hold on to a willow tree growing on the bank, while the rest of us tried to make a chain across the ice-cold stream. This worked well until the third guy had to stand out in the middle of the stream. The pressure from the rapidly flowing stream knocked him off his feet, and we all got swept back to the bank. We tried several times. Each effort proved futile. We were getting hypothermic from the ice-cold water. To add to our frustration, we could see a large plank on the other side of the stream that someone had used to cross the stream, but we had no way of reaching it. Then, Mother Nature decided to chime in. Within 10 minutes, it clouded over and rain began to pour down in buckets. Four tired, soaked, grumpy cold sheep hunters, trudged up the last steep hill to the cabin.

The trail led over the hill, back along the stream, and finally to the old log cabin which was at an altitude of 5000 feet. As quickly as it started the rain stopped; and the sun returned. Now we could see the old cabin and several other out-buildings. We kept noticing blue, pencil shaped, Styrofoam pieces floating down the stream. None of us could figure this phenomenon out. Our welcoming party was the "gold miner in residence"—Charles R. Bilderback. He was not very happy about our arrival, as three other hunters had already beaten us to the cabin. Charlie greeted each one of us with a hearty, bone crushing handshake—asking our name, residence, and occupation. I was the last in line. When I declared that I was a dentist, he went into a half hour long diatribe blaming dentists for the fact that the price of gold was fixed at $35 an ounce. Dentists, he said, had the political clout to influence the price of gold because they used gold to make crowns for their patients. It was a stab in the back to miners to hold the price at $35 per ounce, thus limiting their income. I tried to tell Charlie that President Lyndon B. Johnson or the Congress of the United States was at fault. Not me, nor dentistry. Charlie grumbled about this the entire 10 days we were there. I never got off the hook.

This incredibly beautiful, high remote valley, had seen a lot of mining activity. There were pieces of old horse drawn wagons, and rusting mining equipment, scattered along the stream—even at this 5000-foot altitude. The miners waited for winter, then used teams of horses to pull the heaviest of the equipment up to these high mining areas. I can't imagine such a hard task as that, for both men and horses, considering all the work it took for us to climb up to Charlie's camp. Oh, yes, the blue styrofoam pieces were packaging material from a box containing cartons of milk that Charlie had air-dropped into the camp. The pilot missed the target and the box hit right in front of the cabin and exploded … splashing milk all over the front porch, and then bounced into the creek. No wonder Charlie was in a bad mood when we arrived. Thankfully, he cheered up, when Gordy and I put together a nice dinner.

Early the next morning, Gordy and I had a quick breakfast and headed farther up Dan Creek. It was cold … maybe 28 degrees, and a hard frost covered the ground. We had light packs and our rifles. My rifle was the 7mm Remington I had purchased in Juneau for my first moose hunt near Haines. Gordy had a .264 Magnum that a gunsmith in Portland, Oregon, had custom made for him. He carried it in a special scabbard so as not to get a scratch on it. It was still dark, so we had to use a flashlight to find the trail. Gordy knew where we were going to hunt that day, so he led the way and I followed. The path wound up the creek side for about a mile, then we turned off to follow a smaller tributary stream of Eagle Creek. It took us up to a long, wide valley where Gordy thought we would find the trophy Dall sheep we were seeking. This was the same area where he had taken nine rams in successive years. By now, the sun was rising; but the valley was socked-in with fog. This worked to our advantage as we could move across the valley floor without being spotted by the ever-observant sheep. We were now at about 6000 feet and above the tree line. Willows and lichen were the only vegetation growing there. We climbed up the far side of the valley for about another 300 feet, then we traversed parallel to the valley floor another half-mile. Our packs had to be removed to minimize the noise we were making.

Gordy quietly led us to a large rock outcropping and motioned for me to sit there with him. We sat staring into the thick fog that surrounded us. I had no experience with sheep hunting and was wondering what was going to happen next. It wasn't long before we could hear loud bangs, like two heavy boulders being smacked together. Gordy looked at me, smiling, and gave a thumbs up gesture. I leaned close and asked him what was happening? He said the rams were butting heads as they often do in the rut—part of their ritual competing for the females. This head butting went on for most of the hour we sat there. Finally, the fog began to lift, and just below us at about 100 yards away were six Dall rams. Two were legal trophies, with at least three-quarter curl horns. The four others were too small. You can't imagine the adrenalin rush this scene gave me. I could hardly breathe, and my heartbeat was so strong I thought for sure the rams would hear it. We sat watching for another few minutes while the younger rams continued to butt one another. They backed apart to a distance of 10 or 12 feet, then sort of lift their front legs and charge one another on their hind legs, letting their heads drop to smack their horns together. Apparently, no headaches were produced because they kept repeating the exercise.

Gordy indicated I should follow him and sneak in for a closer shot. We had good cover and got within 75 yards of the sheep. We both agreed as to which of the two larger rams we each should shoot and then found a good shooting position. I could hardly calm down enough to make a steady shot. On the count of three, we fired. Both rams went down and the others scattered. All the dreaming and planning, all the hard work, all the excitement seemed to drain out of me. We congratulated one another and just sat there for 10 or 15 minutes taking it all in. Gordy's success celebration was to have a pinch of snoose (finely-ground-up chewing tobacco), which he put between his lower lip and lower front teeth. I had never tried this nasty trick, but not to be a "party pooper," I took a pinch and joined in the celebration. The snoose activates your salivary glands … so, for the next hour, I was spitting out gross brown balls of saliva. Yuck, reminded me of the card players in Curley Ryan's Saloon in Colon. They could hit a brass spittoon from six feet. I never tried that again.

Now that the glorious part of the hunt was over, it was time for the real work to begin. With Gordy's instruction, I skinned out my ram. We both worked side by side for at least two hours skinning out the rams, being careful around the eyes, nose, and mouth, so as to keep the taxidermist happy with our work. Finally, it was time to head back to camp. We loaded up the horns, cape, and as much meat as we could carry. We would have to return the next day to pack out the remaining meat, provided a bear did not find our cache. I hate packing heavy loads, but the excitement of having shot a three-quarter curl ram over-ruled that complaint. We trudged back to the cabin with our heavy loads. It was a triumphal entry into camp with two legal rams strapped to our back packs. The rest of the hunters gathered around to check out our trophies and offer congratulations. They were eager to hear our stories … and a lot of laughing, and joking, ensued as we embellished our hunting tales. I think most hunters are like that. Charlie was happy … as he needed the meat to make a big pot of delicious sheep stew, which he kept on the stove for several days—adding carrots, onions, and barley as needed. Every hunter's ram contributed to the stew. In order to preserve the rest of the meat to take home, we had to put it in a game bag, sprinkle black pepper all over it, and hang it in the shade. The pepper kept the black flies from ruining the meat.

Charlie Bilderback was one of those unforgettable characters you meet in life. Physically he was a short, bowlegged, partially balding, 68-year-old man. He had been a commercial fisherman from Cape Yakataga, a small community on the west coast of Alaska between Juneau and Cordova. He also had done some commercial logging. He was, we soon discovered, very opinionated. He had perfected the most efficient way to do "everything" … from tying your shoes to halibut fishing by yourself. If Charlie noticed we were not doing something in the most efficient way, he stopped us and gave us a detailed lecture on how we should be tying our shoes, cutting a log, making lamb stew, or clearing rocks from a trail without stopping as we moved along.

I remember one occasion when, for some unknown reason, Charlie brought up the subject of sound wave transmission. We got into a heated conversation about sound waves traveling through water. Charlie insisted that if a frog croaked under water, an air bubble was formed, and inside the rising bubble the croak sound waves bounced around and be released as an audible CROAK when the bubble popped at the surface. I listened to Charlie's unbelievable scientific reasoning. Besides the humor, it brought back childhood memories. So, I told him about when I lived on Palmer Lake in Colon, Michigan, the Day kids spent a lot of time swimming. Kids will be kids; we discovered that if we smacked two rocks together while under water, the sound hurt our ears. If we were standing in shallow water, say three or four feet, we could still hear the sound of the rocks smacking together. So, my scientific conclusion was that sound waves easily traveled through the medium of water. If I burped under water, the bubble did not carry the sound up to those above water and release it when it burst. Further proof was given to me when the German captain of the submarine, *Red October*, in a movie by that name, ordered a "ping" be given to alert the captain of a nearby American submarine.

I related these stories to Charlie to discount his theory and prove my side of the argument. Charlie pounded the table and insisted he had witnessed said frog croaking under water and that he heard said CROAK, emit from the popping bubble. I said, "Charlie, you're full of it." With a sly smile, Charlie wouldn't budge an inch. He was right and I was wrong. That's the way things were with C. R. Bilderback. My way or the highway. Who sits in a cabin at an altitude of 5000 feet, in the magnificent Wrangell Mountains of Alaska, and debates sound wave theory as related to frogs croaking under water? Only one creature in God's creation ... Charles R. Bilderback.

There was a Periodic Table hanging in the back of the cabin. The same one I remember from high school chemistry. At that time, it had 96 elements: gold, silver, hydrogen, sulfur, iron, oxygen, etc. It also included their chemical symbol, atomic weight, atomic number, Brinell hardness, and electron configuration. Charlie sat in a chair with his back to the Periodic Table and asked me to pick out any element. Then without hesitation, he recited to me all the data about that element without missing a single detail. I asked him why he needed to know all that information? He said, very emphatically, that any hard rock miner worth his salt should know all about the chemical elements—especially, the metal elements. I never did figure out why.

The mining claim regulations required that the claim owner have ore samples from the claim assayed each year. Charlie asked Gordy and me to help him carry some of his samples down to the Dan Creek Mine. The following Sunday was warm and sunny, so we loaded up his samples, about 20 pounds each, and headed down the trail to Dan Creek. It was a pleasant hike compared to our hike in, five days before. We got to practice Charlie's lesson on how to kick rocks off the trail without stopping. Needless to say, we heard story after story from Charlie on our way down the trail. I think we made it in about four hours which was two hours better than packing in. We stashed all the ore samples in an old tool shed and headed back to camp. After hunting and climbing around in the mountains for five days, I was in reasonable physical shape and wondered how quickly I could make it back to the cabin. I announced to Charlie and Gordy that I was going to take off and jog back up to the cabin. Much laughter, and "You're nuts!" ensued. I checked my watch and took off on a run. The going was easy on the trail, but hard on the landslide and steep parts, which slowed me down, but I still kept plugging away. On the way out we had reset the board across the stream below the cabin. That saved me significant time. With an empty back pack on a perfect day, it took me two and a half hours to make the trek. That shaved three and a half hours off our hike-in time. I didn't get any accolades from my fellow hunters. No one believed I could do it in that time. So much for "Scouts Honor."

All seven hunters in the camp eventually got their ram. One of the hunters in my group, Ron, was on the heavy side and not in real good physical shape. He hung around camp and didn't hunt very hard. His was the last ram to be taken—a rather pathetic kill. One evening, near the end of our hunt, we were all sitting outside around a fire Charlie had made. Ron still hadn't gotten a shot at a ram, and time was running out. Miracle of miracles. Just as the Lord provided Abraham with a ram to sacrifice, instead of his son Isaac, a lone ram was coming down a nearby ridge. We told Ron, "Wow! There's your ram; go get him." He was hesitant, but we kept up the pressure and he finally grabbed his rifle and ambled off to see if he could get a shot at the unsuspecting ram. It couldn't have been any easier—like shooting fish in a barrel. Within 10 minutes we heard a shot. Gordy took off to help Ron bring the ram in. Just at dark they came in with the most pathetic, sickly, ancient, scraggly, moth-eaten ram I have ever seen. Charlie didn't even want any of the meat for his lamb stew. We counted the annual growth rings on the horns and determined it was at least 12 years old. That's about the lifespan of a wild sheep. It was no spectacular trophy, but Ron was happy and we were happy that he had bagged a sheep. We kidded him that it was probably ready to die anyway. His survival of the coming winter was dooubtful—so Ron did him a favor.

The next day, we said our farewells to Charlie Bilderback and hiked out to the Dan Creek Mine. "Goodbye, Charlie," you crusty old gold miner. "Goodbye, C. R. Bilderback," you old, cantankerous, and opinionated fisherman. "Farewell, Charles R. Bilderback." How we all grew to love you—your opinions, your instructions, your toughness, and the many talents God has given you. Oh, yes, we could see through your toughness. We could see a loving and caring man. God bless you, Charlie Bilderback. I will miss you … especially every time I recall my first sheep hunt. I hope the price of gold goes through the roof.

After 10 days in the mountains, we were all in good physical shape which made the hike out "a walk in the park." Walter Holmes met us at Dan Creek. Then he drove us to the May Creek air strip to meet Mudhole Smith for the flight back to Cordova. We lined up our ram horns and sat leaning against a small log building next to the airstrip trying to sneak in a nap. It was another beautiful, sunny August day, and typical of "bush" flying … all we could do was wait until the plane appeared on the horizon. This could be long and boring; however, not so this day. We were all dozing off when a silver Cessna 180 landed and taxied up to us. Out jumped the pilot and two hunters.

The pilot had a brief chat with his hunters and then flew off. We had a cordial conversation with the hunters and found out that the pilot was the famous bush pilot, Don Sheldon, from Talkeetna. They had hired him as a guide for their sheep hunt. Their hunt so far had been unsuccessful. They were a long way from Talkeetna, but I'm sure Sheldon was familiar with all the good sheep hunting areas and would find them a couple of legal rams. More about the "famous" Don Sheldon later.

Our colorful pilot, Mud Hole Smith, soon arrived, and we happily flew back to Cordova, and on back home to Petersburg. A successful hunt with trophies in hand is so much better than coming home empty-handed.

My Eagle Creek ram.

Charlie Bilderback (middle).

Three Eagle Creek rams.

BILLY GOAT GRUFF

The following fall of 1966, several of my friends and I began making plans to go goat hunting on the mainland across Frederick Sound from Petersburg, an area with plenty of mountain goats. The major determining factor was the weather, which was too often rainy and foggy, making it difficult to hunt. We needed a reasonably calm and sunny day for an ideal hunt. In early December, such a day came along. Four of us piled into Bob Fish's 20-foot boat. It had a small cabin, so we could get out of the weather should a rain storm blow in. We set out just before noon and motored across seven miles of Frederick Sound to what was called Horn Cliffs. These cliffs rose straight up out of the water to about 1000 feet. Bob slowly motored along the cliffs, while the rest of us scoped the mountainside for goats. Within an hour, we spotted three goats at the top of a steep chute. Because of the waves and tides, the boat could not be anchored, so Bob took the three of us to shore to climb the chute and hopefully get a shot at the goats while he tended the boat.

The challenge for us was, as quickly and quietly as possible, to climb up to the goats without spooking them. We figured that we were only going to get one shot. The three of us huffed and puffed our way up the chute—stopping when we had to for a breather. Thankfully we were able to proceed without making too much noise from dislodging the rocks in the chute bed. I think it took us about 20 or 30 minutes to reach a point where we could see the goats. They were standing together, at a distance of about 100 yards, unalarmed that we were visible to them. Our climb had us all breathing rapidly, so we just held steady till everyone calmed down. Each of us selected a goat, and on signal, fired! Two of the goats went down, but the third one just stood there, so I aimed and pulled off a second shot to drop the third goat.

Both male and female goats have horns and I didn't have enough experience to judge from a long distance away exactly what size trophies we had. We climbed to the goats and determined that I had shot a billy and a nanny. The third goat was a nanny. Per usual, in any big game hunt, the hard work starts when the animal is down. We had to gut the goats and get them down the chute to the waiting boat. I took my billy and proceeded to clean out the viscera—okay, guts. The other guys each took a Nanny. They finished sooner than I and took off down to the boat. When I finished the job, I tried to carry the goat down the chute, but he was too heavy. I decided to just drag the carcass down the chute. This proved too slow, so against my better judgment, I decided to sort of push and tumble the goat down the chute. This worked well, but I was worried about ruining the hide and breaking the horns. I finally reached the waiting boat, but my billy's beautiful white cape was now a dull gray, filled with dirt and gravel.

After loading the goats into the boat, we headed back across Frederick Sound, a happy bunch of successful hunters. We took our trophies to a garage where we could wash them off and hang them up to help make the skinning process easier. I have eaten excellent goat ribs, but we did not try the meat from these goats. My billy's horn measurements were enough to just put him in the record book, but more recent larger kills have pushed him out. The taxidermist in Seattle, who had done my Dall sheep, did a beautiful job mounting my goats. They are now my most prized trophies.

Horn Cliffs goats.

Mountain goat country.

LAST CHANCE BEAR

Time was running out and I still wanted to fulfill my big game trophy goals of getting a Brown bear and a black bear before we left for Ann Arbor in August. There were plenty of black bears around Petersburg; so I was confident that I could get a reasonable trophy of that species. Brown bears, however, were a different story. They were not resident on any of the nearby islands. My friend, Gordy Edgars, agreed to take me Brown bear hunting on the west side of Baranof Island. The island's name is taken from Lord Alexander Baranof who was the first Russian Alaska governor in 1799.

Gordy and I chartered a local flying service to take us to a bay that Gordy had selected. Our flight took us about 80 miles northwest of Petersburg. We each had a small tent to sleep in and keep our gear dry. We were in rain country, and there's nothing more miserable than hunting in the rain, but this did not deter us. The area was like Petersburg, with huge stands of Hemlock and Spruce trees. We hunted the area between the forest edge and the tide flats. It was late April, and everything was greening up. Deer and bear came down to the tidal flats to feed on the spring shoots of grass and skunk cabbage.

It was a miracle that we had no rain the three days we were there. Our routine was to have breakfast, then spend the rest of the daylight hours moving along the tide flats and glassing every area where we felt a bear might be. At the beginning of every hunt, our optimism was high, and we could feel the adrenalin flowing. We were sure that the trophy we were hunting would appear any minute.

The first day we saw only a moderate sign of bear scat. The second day was similar, but we did see a large brownie far off across the bay. No chance for a shot at more than 600 yards, and no way to get to him if we did bring him down. Then, we found an ancient bear trail where—for generations—bears had stepped in the same exact spots and worn large circular footprints in the thick moss-covered ground. It is scary to be in Brown bear country, seeing fresh foot prints, fresh scat, knowing they are probably watching us, and one could pop up any moment. "Scary! … Man! … Scary!"

Well, by the end of the third day, we had been skunked. Saw diddly squat, nada, zero, zip. The only hunting time I had left was about three hours before sunset. Gordy was all done … hunted out. I decided to wander back along the forest edge as the remaining light diminished, and the shadows grew longer. I was moseying along about a half mile from camp, just hoping against hope that I might see something. A couple hundred yards ahead, where the spring grass met the forest, I could see more than a dozen Sitka black-tailed deer feeding. I slowly poked along getting closer to the deer, but they just kept feeding and didn't seem to mind my being there. I kept looking and glassing ahead of me in the evening shadows along the forest edge. It was very quiet … not a breath of wind. I was about to give up when I thought I saw some movement along the trees about 150 yards ahead. I quickly took cover in the tall grass and scoped the spot. Sure enough, there was not one, but two Brown bears slowly walking my way. One had a very dark coat and the other was a lighter brown. My guess was that they were twins. Strategy, strategy, what should I do? I don't want two bears, just one, and I was running out of light. Gordy, old experienced bear hunter, where are you when I need you? He was back at camp drinking coffee or maybe taking a nap or a nip.

I had borrowed the rifle I was using. It was a very old, lever-action Winchester with an octagonal barrel and open sites. I can't remember the caliber, but it was up to the task. I took it out to the dump in Petersburg and shot it a few times before we left and felt confident I could hit any target at 200 yards or less. Well, I had to do something. It was now or never. There was a small tidal slough between me and the bears. I had hip boots on, but didn't know how deep it was. I crouched down, then walked slowly toward the bears and down into the slough. It was about 25 yards across. Fortunately, it was only about three feet deep at that stage of incoming tide. I knew that when I reached the far side and climbed up the bank, I would be about 75 yards from the bears. It was a godsend that there was tall grass for cover as I climbed up the bank for a last look. My heart was pounding as I rose up to see where the bears were. They were feeding on the spring skunk cabbage no more than 75 yards away, and hadn't seen me, or gotten a whiff of my scent. The deer that I was worried about spooking the bears, had just quietly faded back into the forest.

I crouched down to calm myself a bit and take the safety off the rifle. Then I slowly stood up and took aim at the closest bear. POW! He went down and the other bear spun around and headed for the forest. I took a second shot, as the bear I had hit had gotten up. Now, as my target bear went down a second time, the other bear, about 100 yards away, spun back around and began running towards me. My brain was racing … I was thinking the bear doesn't know where I am, but he's heading right for me. I didn't want to shoot it, so when the bear was about 50 yards away, I lifted the rifle over my head and yelled as loud as I could, waving the rifle and my arms to scare him off. The bear stopped about 35 yards from me, rose up on his hind legs, looked me in the eye, then turned and ran back into the forest. Was I glad? Was I happy? Was I scared? You bet. You bet!

Now, of course, I have a bear to skin. It's twilight, and the other bear is in the adjacent forest. I thought, well, I'll skin the bear till I have just enough light left to get back to camp, then return in the morning at first light to finish the job. All went well except for when I had to have my back to the forest where the second bear had gone. I could picture him coming back, angry, and wanting to get revenge for what I had done to his partner. At last, I accomplished as much skinning as I could, and then headed back to camp to tell Gordy of my success. He was happy that I had got a "last chance" bear.

Early the next morning we hustled to the skinning task so we could get back to camp before our plane landed to take us back to Petersburg. Then, just as we finished breaking camp, the plane landed, and we headed home. We were both looking forward to a hot shower and a comfortable bed that night.

The next day I salted the hide, packed it into a garbage can, and shipped it off to the taxidermist in Seattle. Later that week I went into Fish and Game to report my kill. The game warden asked, "Where's your bear skin? I need to measure it." I told him I had shipped it off to Seattle. He seemed rather miffed. The result was that I had to have the hide shipped back, and in addition he fined me $75.00. Of course, this infraction of the law was published in our local paper, "The Petersburg Pilot." "Local dentist fined $75.00 for illegal handling of bear hide." I was embarrassed by the publishing of my minor crime in the community paper. The local gossips had a heyday at my expense. Life goes on ... you win some, and you lose some.

HI BEAR. HO BEAR. HEY BEAR.

With my Brown bear tag filled, it was now time to find a decent black bear. I had sold the river punt that I had built a couple years earlier, so I decided to charter Lon's Flying Service for the short flight to Duncan Canal. This was a good area for spring black bear hunting, and the Forest Service had a cabin with a small boat and motor I could rent. This time ... I hunted with my own Remington Model 94 lever-action 30.30 which was adequate to take a black bear. I motored slowly along the shore and into various bays and coves. The bears here, as on Baranof Island, were out feeding on the newly sprouted skunk cabbage and spring grass. I spotted four bears by noon, but they all seemed too small and I passed on taking a shot. It was lunch time, so I pulled into a small stream bed for a lunch break and began reading my *Time* magazine. I occasionally looked about with my binoculars to see if a blackie chose to present himself for me to evaluate. I didn't have to wait long. At about a distance of 600 yards, I spotted a good- size bear coming out of the forest onto the tide flats to join me for lunch. I was totally exposed and there was not much cover to choose from. I surmised it was time for some real "strategery," a useful word President George Bush invented. I secured the skiff as best as I could. The tide was going out, so I had at least six hours before it would be coming in and float my boat away. I put on my backpack, grabbed my rifle, and dropped down into the stream bed for cover. The only way I was going to get close enough for a decent shot was to follow the stream up to its exit from the forest, and then sneak through the forest till I was opposite the bear. I crept along all hunched over, taking a peek at the bear every 50 yards or so. He was enjoying his skunk cabbage snack and not aware of my presence. I entered the forest and was surprised to find that the spruce trees and alders were growing on huge boulders the size of a pickup truck. This made the going rough. I had to remove my backpack because I was making too much noise. I slowly made my way along until I was close to where the bear had come out of the forest. My guess was that I was about 75 yards from him. I had the cover of the forest, and he was totally out in the open. Everything was to my advantage except for the usual increase in heart beat and adrenaline flow that always accompanies this part of the stalk. I found a tree branch that was the right height for a rest and drew a bead on Mr. Bear. POW! He stood up and looked around. POW! He dropped down on all fours and began heading right for me. POW! POW! POW! Now he was coming into the forest about 35 yards away from me. I hadn't touched a hair on his body. He bounded right up onto a nearby boulder pile and stopped to look around. The wind was in my favor, so he didn't know I was so close to him. My heart was pounding and felt like it was about to come out of my chest. I thought, *five shots and I haven't touched him. My sights must be off, way off.* It was time for one more quick shot. I found another small branch to steady my sighting and squeezed off another shot. Unbelievable. Much to my surprise … the bear dropped right to the ground. He didn't even take one step. This was crazy.

After five shots and no resultant success, I couldn't understand how I had dropped the bear with one shot. I waited … and waited … and waited … for him to jump up and run off. Eventually, I decided to throw rocks at him, thinking he might still be alive.. He never moved. After 15 more minutes, I crept over to where I could poke him with a large stick, but still, no sign of life. Finally, I got brave enough to closely check the bear out but still couldn't even find a wound. *He must have died of a heart attack,* I said to myself. Then, as I tried to roll the bear over, I placed my hand on his head. It was soft as opposed to a normal hard skull. My shot had gone right into his ear and literally exploded his skull. No wonder he just dropped. Okay, okay, it was just a lucky shot; but you'll admit that it was just what I needed at that point.

Now I was back to bear skinning again, packing the hide, and heading out to my waiting skiff. It was a good day, a successful hunt, albeit a bit scary. I can't seem to bring a bear down without it running at me. Maybe you could invite me on a pheasant, rabbit, or duck hunt sometime. That would be much safer and provide a tasty meal.

PART IV

STARTING ALL OVER

ROUND TRIP

The good news, actually the miraculous news, came that I had been accepted as a graduate student in Michigan's orthodontic program. I was an above average dental student. I graduated in the upper third of my class in the operatory clinic and was awarded a Michigan Dental License without having to take the Michigan State Dental Board examination. But with the odds of being accepted into the orthodontic program of 8 out of 180 applicants, the deck was obviously stacked against me. I've always wondered if Dr. Aldrich swung the pendulum in my favor? Did we see the hand of the Lord at work here? Yes! Proverbs 16:9 "A man's heart plans his way, but the Lord directs his steps."

We sold our house and dental practice in Petersburg in August of 1967. We loaded all our belongings into the bed of our new red Chevy pickup that I had bought in Portland and stuffed everything else into the little VW Bug that we towed. Then, Sali and I along with little Holly and Heather made the long drive to Ann Arbor, Michigan, for two years of dental school in Orthodontics. This was my eighth and ninth year of university education.

We bought a new house in Ann Arbor and found reasonably priced furniture in a store on the west side of Detroit. Don't ask me how. Another miracle of God's provision was going on and I didn't even see it.

Sali enrolled at Eastern Michigan University and did modeling for Wagner's, a popular campus clothing store in Ann Arbor. Holly, almost seven, went to a nearby grade school, and Heather, at four, was not in school yet. It was a blessing to have my mother-in-law, Mimi, live with us to take care of both our girls.

The time flew by, and two years later with my Orthodontic degree in hand, we were loading up a 20-foot "Dunrite Insulation" van that my brother Jim had found in Detroit and fixed up for our move to Anchorage, Alaska. By this time, we had acquired a baby grand piano that had belonged to Sali's mother. It took four of us to lift and load the piano. We stood it on its side and wrapped it in blankets. I had this traumatic vision of the bumpy ride of 3800 miles up the ALCAN Highway rendering my mother-in law's precious gift into a pile of splinters. I should mention that by this time our marriage already had some big splinters in it.

My younger brother, Bob, and two college friends, volunteered to drive the van up to Alaska. I purchased a trailer to tow behind our pickup. We loaded up all our material possessions and made our own "Alaska or Bust" caravan. The boys in the "five miles per gallon" van, took off early in the morning. We usually caught up with them parked along the highway, sitting on top of the van like three big birds … and out of gas. I had a 5-gallon can of gas to get them to the next gas station. It was a long, 13-day… but fun, trip. Our budget was limited, so we lived on peanut butter and jelly sandwiches every day.

We rolled into Anchorage August 9, 1969. Now we needed to find a house and get Holly and Heather enrolled in grade school. We found a small new house in a nice neighborhood near an elementary school and settled in.

I had intended to seek an associateship with one of the three Anchorage orthodontists. It just so happened that one of the orthodontists was in the hospital for removal of a brain tumor and his wife asked if I would take his practice until he recovered. Of course, I was agreeable

to this offer. Following this, I practiced with another established orthodontist for a year. I then began my own practice. I was orthodontist number '4' in private practice in Alaska at last.

Kenai River King.

Return to Alaska.

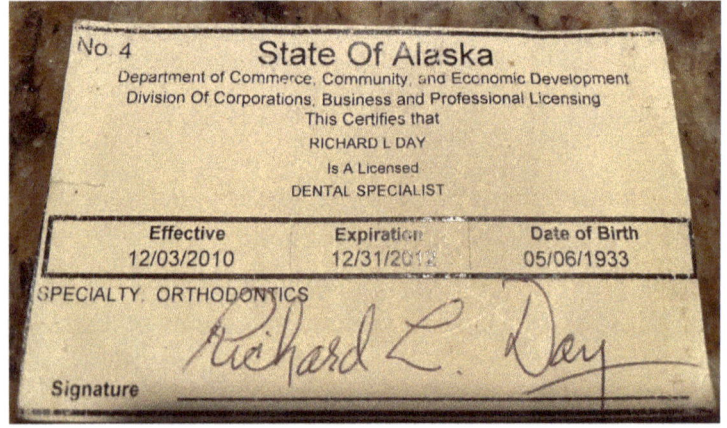

A HARVARD HUNTER

In 1971, our second year in Anchorage, I sensed the high, and lonesome valley of Eagle Creek calling me to return to the Wrangell Mountains. I had become friends with Floyd Smith, a Harvard graduate and an Anchorage attorney. I decided to invite him on a sheep hunt. He readily accepted. We then made plans for the trip to Chitina where we usually caught up with our bush pilot, Howard Knutsen.

Chitna, or what was left of it, was a wide space at the end of the road. It dated back to the railroad-building days and the opening of the

Kennicott Mine in early 1900. Once a bustling place, it was now only a bar, gas station, post office, and small grocery store.

Howard had the reputation of being an excellent bush pilot and sheep hunting guide. Howard's wife was the postmistress—that's probably the only reason they lived in Chitna. When Floyd and I met him, he pointed out a male wolf pup he had found and was trying to domesticate. The pup was held in a large pen. Howard said I was welcome to go inside the pen and make friends with the wolf pup. I strolled over to the pen fence, took a look at this almost full-sized male wolf, and decided not to enter the pen as Howard said I could; I needed my fingers to do orthodontics.

I asked Howard to fly me to Charlie Bilderback's high Eagle Creek cabin to airdrop our food and sleeping bags into the alders behind the cabin. This went well, as we hit the target in two runs. It saves an enormous amount of heavy packing to deliver our camping gear in this fashion. It also allows us to have a few luxuries like butter, jam, milk, bacon, plenty of pancake mix, and Blazo fuel for a lantern. We didn't want to pack all that on our back for the six miles to the cabin.

I should mention that, on our flight between Chitina and Dan Creek, Howard spotted a large grizzly bear trying to take down a bull moose. The bear ran alongside the moose then raised his paws as high as he could and brought them down on the back of the moose, attempting to break its spine. Howard dove his Cub straight for the bear, pulled up, made a tight turn, and dove again. This caused the grizzly to stop his pursuit of the moose. The grizzly got angry at our dive bombing, and stood up on his hind legs pawing the air at us. Meanwhile, Mr. Moose sped away. We distracted the bear for 10 or 15 minutes, then we headed for the cabin. I don't know whether the moose got safely away or not. I doubt it, because the bear could certainly follow his scent. C'est la vie! Mother Nature is not always kind to her children.

Howard dropped me off at the Dan Creek strip, and left to pick up Floyd. Before we headed for the cabin, I gave Floyd a tour around the Dan Creek Mine. Now, seven years after my first hunt, several more of the buildings had collapsed, and the few that remained were not safe to enter. Only a machine shop stood against the ravages of time and decay. It may have been because of the preservative nature of oil, gasoline and other petroleum products used there. An old bulldozer, oil barrels, and a few large tool parts that were too large for scavengers to cart off, were all that remained.

We shouldered our backpacks, and headed for the trail up Dan Creek. I told Floyd how Dean Weeden, on the previous hunt, had found a nice gold nugget in the stream bedrock and to keep his eyes open for such a treasure. Our luck wasn't as good, and nary a speck of gold did we see.

The steep bank with the hanging rope was still there some seven years later. This was the hardest physical part of the hike, maybe 40 feet straight up. The weather was exactly the same as on my first hunt; a clear, sunny, almost hot, early August day in the Wrangell Mountains. Our pace was about one mile an hour, the same pace that our hunting party had made before, and of course, just as before, it poured down rain during our last mile to the cabin. I had to use a flashlight to find the trail for the final push to the Bilderback cabin. We were soaking wet and very tired but still elated as we climbed the porch steps and entered the dry shelter.

I lit an old Coleman lantern which allowed us to see the shambles in the cabin. The ground squirrels had found their way through the floorboards and chewed into rice, flour, beans, anything that wasn't in a plastic or metal container.

I took my trusty flashlight outside into the alders behind the cabin to find our airdropped gear. Everything was in good shape except for Floyd's sleeping bag. The double plastic bag into which we had stuffed it, had caught on an alder branch and was torn open leaving the bag exposed to the rain. It was pretty well soaked. Fortunately, there were enough old blankets in the cabin under which Floyd could sleep. The only other problem we had was that Floyd's new, stiff, hiking boots had caused huge blisters on each heel. I doctored him up with A&D ointment and band aids.

The next morning was gray and cold. Floyd decided to spend the day cleaning up the cabin and organizing things in camp. This would give his Olympic blisters a chance to heal. I decided to head up toward Eagle Creek to poke around and see if any sheep were in the area. I hiked up Dan Creek about half a mile to where Eagle Creek flowed into it, then turned north to follow it up stream. It was only 8 to 10-feet wide at this point and the gravel bars made the slow ascent easy. The previous two times I had gone this route with my friend Gordy, I noticed another small feeder stream flowing out of a narrow canyon. My curiosity got the best of me—and I decided to follow that stream into the unexplored canyon. I was just poking along, taking my time, climbing and scoping the area hoping to see a nice ram. Back along Dan Creek I had seen bear scat, and again I noticed a few more piles along this stream, so I thought I might see a grizzly. The only one we had previously seen was a very small bear near the headwaters of Dan Creek—not a trophy anyone wanted.

The weather remained cold, cloudy, and ominous. The narrow valley I had entered was barren of any vegetation. It had high, vertical walls and scattered large boulders on the floor where I was walking. Snow began to fall, not hard but steady enough to obscure the distant mountains. The snow melted on the rocky floor turning everything wet and gray. Eventually I could see that I had entered a box canyon and decided that there was no point going any further. As I stood there, just looking around, it became obvious that this was a spooky, eerie, and very dead place. There wasn't a living thing here except for me. It reminded me of the habitat of Gollum in Tolkien's *Hobbit* trilogy. I was expecting the slimy and ugly character to poke his head out of one of the small pools on the canyon floor. I could hear a voice saying to me, "Get out of here; get out of here." That's what I did. I spun around and headed back to the cabin. Within 45 minutes, I was at the cabin enjoying a cup of hot coffee with Floyd. For some unknown reason I did not discuss "Gollum's Valley" with Floyd, in fact this is the first time I have ever mentioned it. A mysterious place best left alone.

The second day of the hunt, we went up into Eagle Creek Valley. It was another beautiful day to hike and hunt. There was new snow at the

7,000-foot elevation which had accumulated the day before. We spent the day scoping out every area that sheep might be grazing. We hiked up into the far end of the valley where we could see Pyramid Peak, and lots of beautiful scenery, but no sheep. It is rare to not see sheep in this area. We did spook a flock of ptarmigan out of the willows. It's a startling experience to be quietly walking along and suddenly a loud whir of wings fills the air. Our reaction was to take quick aim, feinting a 12-gauge shot. "Don't worry birds, you are safe!" I had wanted to find Floyd a nice trophy ram but no such luck. All of the planning, hiking, and effort expended for naught. Hunting is like that—sometimes you win, sometimes you lose. Here, high in the Wrangell Mountains, you always win. The awesome beauty that surrounded us: the frosty mornings, early snowfall, sunrises and sunsets, scenery I have no words to describe, rushing mountain streams, distant flocks of sheep

grazing on the mountain side, are all trophies worth the hard work to see, even if we bring nothing home. All good things must come to an end; so the next morning, we packed up and headed back down to the Dan Creek Mine for our flight back to Chitina.

ALASKA'S DARING BUSH PILOT

The same year I took Floyd Smith sheep hunting, I received a call from a dental friend, Jim Carlson. Jim practiced nearby in Palmer and wanted to go moose hunting during the November season. Alaska used to have September and November moose seasons.

Jim said he would contact Don Sheldon in Talkeetna and hire him to fly us out to a good moose hunting area. You will recall my first encounter with Don Sheldon at the May Creek landing strip. We had just finished a very successful sheep hunt near Charlie Bilderback's cabin in the Wrangell Mountains and were waiting for Mud Hole Smith to pick us up. Sheldon landed with two hunters he was guiding. They came over, introduced themselves, and admired our trophies.

I had no knowledge of Don Sheldon's fame. He was Alaska's most renowned bush pilot—a legend of the skies. He survived WWII as a B-17 Flying Fortress tail gunner, where life expectancy was about zero. He received the Distinguished Flying Cross for his service.

At age 17, Don arrived in Alaska. He worked in Anchorage for a while, then made his way to Talkeetna. After WWII he returned to Talkeetna, and he and a partner formed Talkeetna Air Service in 1947. Over the next 28 years, Don pioneered high altitude glacier landings on nearby Denali (Mt. McKinley), performed miraculous rescues of mountain climbers, military members, downed aircraft with injured passengers, stranded hunters or fishermen, and people in remote places in need of medical help. He had a room full of citations, but never sought any praise or adoration. Many of these stories are recorded in a book, *Wager with the Wind* by James Greiner. I highly encourage you to purchase it and enjoy the read. I regret not having any knowledge about our pilot before he flew us out from Talkeetna to go moose hunting.

Talkeetna is a small town on the Susitna River, about 100 miles north of Anchorage on the way to Fairbanks. It was a prominent town back in the 1920's during the construction of the railroad between Seward and Fairbanks. Today it is still a small town known primarily as the staging point for Denali climbers and as a tourist destination. It was noted also for their "Moose Dropping Festival," to which PETA objected , thinking they were dropping a live moose in the festivities. No, the droppings were authentic dried moose poop! The festival has since been canceled however, due to too much drinking and rowdy behavior. Another attraction for visitors was Stubbs—a yellow and orange cat, with the title of "honorary mayor" for 20 years. Best of all, on a clear day, Talkeetna offers a spectacular view of Denali, North America's highest mountain, 20,310 feet high.

Jim and I rolled up to Don's Talkeetna Air Service hanger with all our camping and hunting gear. Don put me in the back of his Super Cub. Then he proceeded to load up my lap with boxes of our food and gear. By the time he was done, the boxes reached the ceiling of the plane. Sheldon jumped in, fired up the engine, and off we flew to an unknown hunting spot.

We headed west to the Yenlo Mountains, some 40 or 50 miles. During the flight as Don spotted a moose, he banked the plane to one side or the other and said, "There's a moose," or "There's a couple moose," or "There's a big Bull!" My excitement grew as Don pointed out moose after moose. As we approached our destination, Don pointed out a clearing where he could land if it was closer to where we might shoot a moose.

Don landed on an airstrip belonging to the Sunflower Creek Mine. He taxied to the north end of the strip where he unloaded all our boxes and me. Then off he flew back to Talkeetna to pick up Jim. I had our tent, so I began to clear an area of deep snow and put it up. Only willows and a few small spruce trees grew in this area.

A couple hours later, Don returned with Jim and the rest of our gear. We got our camp organized and decided to go over and check out the miner's house which was mid-way down the airstrip. It was a weathered two-bedroom building with a covered porch all along the front. As we got closer to the house, we could see a large sign attached to the door. It read:

BEWARE

DYNAMITE

IF YOU OPEN THIS DOOR

YOU ARE

DEAD

We decided to let sleeping dogs sleep … and went back to our tent. The sun was setting and it was about 15 degrees outside, so we had the bright idea of having dinner in the tent. We lit our Coleman lantern and stove. This proved to be a stupid move. The heat inside the tent and the 15 degree temperature outside caused it to rain in the tent. The accumulated moisture on the inside of the tent then froze so—we slept in an igloo for the rest of our hunt. Not good … not good … so, our meals from then on were cooked outside at any temperature.

The next morning, we quickly dressed in our cold tent. We melted snow to make coffee, and we had a dry bagel and some trail mix for breakfast.

The deep snow required us to hunt on snowshoes. We headed out in the direction of the clearing where Don said he could land. It was a cloudless sunny day, with a temperature of 25 degrees. From the clearing, we headed south on rolling terrain with patches of willows. The mile trek in deep snow was slow, but there were plenty of moose tracks to encourage us.

I don't think we had hunted more than two hours when we spotted a group of five bulls. Two were legal, and the other three were young bulls—safe from our intentions. We had plenty of cover and a favorable wind. We closed the distance between us and the bulls to about 75 yards. There was no need to choose one bull over the other as they looked to have about the same size antlers. We each agreed on our target and took our shots. Both bulls went down and the rest scattered. Jim had a clean kill, but I had to take a second shot to complete the task. We exchanged our high fives, chatted a bit, and got to the long task of gutting and quartering our kills.

Our next adventure was to tie a rope around a leg of a quarter and proceed to drag it on the snowshoe trail we had made back to the clearing where Don said he could land. This made it easier than creating a new trail. The rest of the afternoon was spent getting all the moose quarters to the clearing.

We were standing by our pile of moose meat when we heard the drone of an approaching plane. *Perfect timing*, we thought. Don had come to check on us. He circled and tossed out a small cardboard tube. Down it tumbled, over and over, and landed out in the clearing. We retrieved it. Inside was a message: "Sorry, can't land there. Take moose to airstrip." Don waggled his wings and flew off to a warm bed in Talkeetna. Reminded me of the jet pilots that flew over our heads on our North Star maneuver in my Army days.

We grumbled and complained a bit, then headed back the mile to our camp at the Sunflower Creek Mine airstrip. It was twilight, and we had had a long hard day. Tomorrow, our task was to drag the meat to the airstrip. We fixed some sort of dinner, crawled into our sleeping bags, and discussed our successful hunt until we fell asleep.

Jim's watch alarm woke us at first light. We had another exciting cold breakfast, except for the coffee. Our thought was that if we could move all the quarters to the airstrip by early afternoon, then Don could fly us and our meat into Talkeetna before dark. We had a frozen trail on which to drag the quarters which enabled us to make good time, and we were able to reach our goal.

With perfect timing, Don came to check on us and was able to do what we had hoped. Now, back in Talkeetna, we loaded up Jim's truck and headed for Palmer. A successful hunt brings good feelings and excitement about doing another one!

The following year, we decided to repeat our November moose hunt. Jim made all the arrangements with Don. We arrived in Talkeetna on a Thursday and planned to hunt for the next three days. This time we knew we were to hunt again in the Yenlo Mountains. This time, Don chose a different area in the Yenlo Mountains for us to hunt.

We flew in his Cessna 180 this time—with lots of power and speed … and no box blocking my view. Don selected a long clearing to land on, thinking that we might have a heavier load on our return flight. He agreed to pick us up late in the afternoon on Sunday. We set up our tent and spent the rest of the day checking out the area near our camp for moose sign—to no avail.

The next day, we hunted on snowshoes from first light until almost sunset, with no success. We only saw a couple cows with their yearlings in the distance, and were startled by a flock of whirring ptarmigan that we spooked.

Saturday, we got up at daylight and hunted until almost dark in a different area, and we were skunked. We saw nothing more than an occasional raven flying over. At a higher altitude, Alaska Air flights were going to and from Anchorage to Fairbanks.

Now, it was Sunday … our last chance to bring some moose meat home. We hunted till midafternoon and hadn't seen one legal bull. Perhaps hunters in the September season had diminished the bulls in this area. We were hunted out, and it was time to head back to camp and pack up our gear in readiness for Don's arrival.

Each day had been clear, cold, and sunny. The Yenlo's are just south of Denali and offer fantastic views of North America's tallest mountain. Measured from base to summit, Denali is taller than Mount Everest. This glorious mountain of 20,310 feet was within our view each day of our hunt. Every day we would pause to soak in this pinnacle wonder of God's creation. Denali stands as an ever-observant Sentinel, offering a challenge of victory, defeat, and sometimes death, to those who attempt to climb her. Though our hunting goal was not reached, we were content with Denali's magnificent daily display.

Sunset in this part of Alaska in November is about 4:30 p.m. We were all packed and ready for Don. As it began to get dark, we decided to tramp out a runway with our snowshoes. This gave us something to do as well as warmed us up. While we tramped down the snow, we expected Don to arrive any minute. Now it was almost 6 p.m. … and no Don. Our hopes of being picked up and sleeping in a warm bed that night were waning. We discussed having to put our tent back up.

It was a still, moonlit night … I lit our Coleman Lantern and placed it at the far end of our snowshoed runway. Suddenly! The silence was interrupted by the welcome prop noise of Don's beautiful Cessna 180. With his landing lights on, Don skillfully put the plane down in full darkness, taxied up to us, and spun the plane around. I ran down to grab our lantern, then we loaded up our gear, climbed in, and happily flew back to Talkeetna with Sheldon.

To Jim and me, it was a miracle to watch Don fulfill his promise to us, and land in the dark. To Don, who had made hundreds of dangerous landings, it probably was all in a day's work. Jim and I discussed our hunt, our flights, and of course, our pilot, as we drove through the night back to Palmer. Jim was much more knowledgeable than I about Don's exploits … but since our last hunt I had read a great deal about Don Sheldon's bush pilot heroics.

Don only lived about another two years after our second hunt … due to cancer. I was saddened by his early death, and I thought about the many times he had faced death and defeated it during his adventurous bush pilot career. Don gave greatly of himself to risk his life to save others, without expecting any kind of reward or acclamation. Looking back, I am so glad I had the privilege of flying with Alaska's famous and daring Bush Pilot Hero … Don Sheldon.

Don Sheldon, Alaska's famous bush pilot.
Photo credit: The Sheldon family of Talkeetna, Alaska.

Don Sheldon's Piper Cub aircraft with wheel-skis. Photo credit: The Sheldon family of Talkeetna, Alaska.

Loading Don Sheldon's super-charged Cessna 180 on Mt. Denali Photo credit: Jim Thuot.

Mount Denali (McKinley), North America's highest peak; 20,310 feet.

Photo credit: Jeff Bonin.

SWEET INVESTMENT—SOUR LESSON

After practicing orthodontics for about five years, I had a new office and Sali and I were having our dream home built near the office. All was quiet on the western front.

The time seemed right to make an investment or two. My understanding of the buying and selling of stocks was minimal. The terms, "puts, calls, selling short, call spread," and my favorite, "short sale against the box," all were mysteries to me.

One morning I had a phone call at my office. Upon answering, I heard a very enthusiastic voice with a heavy New York accent: "Doctor Day! Doctor Day! This is Jacques Wiseman! I'm a broker from British American Commodities! Have you heard of us?"

"No," I replied.

"Well, Doctor Day … I have exciting news for you. Are you familiar with the Commodities Market?"

I replied "No."

Jacques went on, "The price of sugar today is at rock bottom … it's never been lower and it can only go up. You can tie up (X) metric tons of sugar for only $7,500. It's almost guaranteed that you will make a lot of money. I highly recommend that you make this investment."

I mulled over the offer. I was looking for something to invest in and I had the money. Jacques had thrown out the bait and now he was waiting to set the hook. With no knowledge of the Commodity Market and the risky bet I was making, I took the bait. Now I'm into sugar … tons of sugar. I could see the money rolling in. Such a deal. Such a deal. Time to order a new Porsche.

A couple weeks later my phone rings. "Doctor Day! Doctor Day! It's Jacques Wiseman. How are you today?" "Just fine Jacques, just fine. How's my sugar doing?"

"Oh, Doctor Day, things are going very well, very well! I'm calling to offer you another (X) metric tons of sugar at the same price of $7,500. We expect you to double your money within the next year. I'm telling you, this is a great deal. You won't go wrong with this investment."

I was hooked again. I, a dentist, had forgotten that sugar rots your teeth.

My memory is a bit fuzzy as to the exact dates, but within the next six months, British American Commodities went belly up—Bankrupt! Jacques didn't call me to report the news or express his condolences. I took it upon myself to call him. We had a rather stressful conversation. I informed him that if I could reach through the phone line, I'd put my hands around his neck and strangle him! Jacques was highly offended by my statement. "Doctor Day, how could you possibly feel that way, such anger! These things happen, it's not my fault!" The end result was that I lost $15,000!

The lesson I learned was: It's wise to thoroughly research your potential investment. Talk to an investment advisor, a stock broker, or someone you trust who invests. I'd have been better off putting my money in a box under the bed until I had enough to buy the farm I've always wanted. My experience in a lifetime of investing, I'm sorry to say, has been poor to tragic. C'est la vie.

A WORLD RECORD

A year or two after I took Floyd Smith sheep hunting … my friend and fellow dentist, Tom Redmond, wanted me to be his guide on another sheep hunt in the Wrangell Mountains. I'm sure my hunting stories fostered this request. So, the planning began. We gave Howard Knutsen a call and arranged for our flight into Dan Creek.

All the groceries and gear were assembled and loaded into the back of my Chevy pickup. Tom and I then left for Chitina some 200 miles away on a beautiful August day.

Howard flew me up to the Bilderback cabin to air-drop our supplies. While we were in the area, Howard and I flew over several nearby valleys to spot for sheep. Not far from the cabin we spotted a legal ram and two ewes. If they stayed where they were, I knew Tom would have a chance to take this nice ram.

Howard dropped me off at the Dan Creek airstrip and went on back to Chitina to pick up Tom. While I waited for them to return, I wandered through the silent and decaying camp trying to visualize the men and horses of long ago as they mined the hidden gold.

We had a perfect, yet very warm day, to hike into the cabin. Our trek in was uneventful. It still took six hours to cover the six miles and a lot of sweating. The cabin, as always, was at the mercy of the ground squirrels. We spent an hour cleaning up their mess and organizing our gear. After a good dinner, I took out our map and showed Tom where the ram had been. We planned the route of our stalk and hit the sack. The adrenalin generated by thoughts of tomorrow's hunt made it hard to fall asleep.

We awoke to another beautiful day. I was confident that Tom had a good chance to get a shot at a nice Dall ram today. I led the way up Dan Creek, into the morning sun. We turned north to follow Eagle Creek and a smaller stream coming out of the valley. This was going to be an easy stalk because we had covered all the way to a spot where we would be above the sheep. Now it was, as the old guides call it, "Go and Blow" time. We had to climb up a steep incline for about 100 yards. Tom and I were in our early 40's and not in great shape, but we trudged away and reached the top of the ridge with minimal pain. There was no hurry, so we unloaded our packs and took a break. The breathing rate and heart beats went down, but the adrenalin rush increased. I was thinking that just over that ridge and below us should be the ram and his brides.

I explained to Tom what I expected him to see when we peeked over the ridge. At a snail's pace we pushed forward to get into position for him to take a shot. Of course, the sheep could have been long gone in the 24 hours that had lapsed since Howard and I flew over them. As we peered over the ridge, about 75 yards below us were the two ewes standing next to the beautiful ram. He was lying on the shale enjoying the warm sunshine, totally unaware of our presence. He was easily a legal ram with a better than three quarter curl to his horns. I whispered to Tom, "It's now or never." He found a good steady position and squeezed off a shot. The ram never moved. He just settled into an infinite nap. The ewes took off and were soon out of sight. Time for congratulations, hurrah, and high fives. I think we took a nip from a flask that Tom just happened to have along to sterilize any wounds we might incur.

We had to backtrack down, and around, and up into the area where the ram lay. As usual, now began the gutting, skinning, and cutting up of the meat ... then packing it back to camp. This took us several hours. By mid-afternoon, we were back at the cabin salting the hide, and hanging the meat in a cool place. I knew Tom was happy about his success, and enjoying that euphoric feeling that goes with such a hunting accomplishment.

Now it was my turn to find a legal ram for my "man cave." The next morning, in perfect weather, I led Tom up into my favorite place, Eagle Creek Valley. We followed along the edge of the creek side, with willows for cover, up into the west end of the valley. The valley stretched east for almost a mile, with lichens, moss, and willows covering the valley floor. The head waters of Eagle Creek were at the valley's end. This is where I shot my first ram. There were small rivulets streaming down from the higher elevations and groups of large boulders scattered along their length. It was a favorite place for the sheep to feed. Tom and I remained in the willows and began to scope the north slope which was in full sunlight. It only took us a couple minutes to spot a flock of sheep. They were above us across the valley floor and a bit east of us— probably a little more than 200 yards away. I counted three rams and four ewes, all adults, no lambs. I checked out the rams and all seemed to be legal. Tom said that I should take a closer look at the largest ram. Finding a ram with a full curl, or greater, was a rare occasion. However, there, in this small flock, was a ram with at least a full curl and I'd bet even a bit more. A once in a lifetime opportunity was presenting itself to me.

Tom and I had a pow wow. We agreed on some hand signals to enable him to tell me what the sheep were doing ... going up, going down, staying in place. He would lay hidden in the shade of the willows as I made my stalk. I planned to look back at Tom through my scope to see his hand signals responding to what the sheep were doing. The only choice I had was to cross the open valley floor in a direct line toward the sheep. There was no cover. I had read about a hunter in a similar situation. He cautioned to walk very slowly with your hat brim pulled down to hide your face, keeping your gaze just ahead of your steps. I had no idea if this would work, but what else could I do?

The adrenalin and excitement level in me made it hard to stand … let alone move along in full view of the sheep. I started out very slowly, crouched over, and in a direct line with the sheep. Eventually, as I moved closer to the north slope of the valley, I got under the sheep's line of vision and could move faster. I chose a small gulley to climb that kept me out of sight, about 50 yards west of the sheep. When I gained some altitude above the valley floor, I glanced back to check the hand signals from Tom. "The best laid schemes of mice o' men Gang aft a-gley, An' lea'e us naught but grief an' pain, For promised joy!" (A little Robert Burns for you.) Tom was in the willow shadows, and even with my 10-power rifle scope, I could not see his signal, nor could I tell him so. RATS! I kept climbing until I thought I was as high as the sheep. Now to just crawl slowly up out of the gully for a peek and Mr. World Record Ram should be right there. With a pounding heart I pulled myself along on my belly, keeping my 7mm ready for a shot. There I was, and what did I see? NOTHING, NOTHING! Not a sheep in sight. I got out my binoculars and began glassing the slope; no sheep anywhere. I decided to scope out the valley floor from which I had just come. There they were, straight down, and a little up the valley floor from me, drinking from the midvalley stream.

My quick assessment of the situation was that I could follow the gully back down towards the valley floor and try to get a closer shot or just try a shot from where I was. I chose the latter. I had no experience with taking a 45-degree downhill, 125-yard shot, and it was too late now to try to compute my aim compensation, high or low? I found the best position I could, and located the big ram in my scope. The tall willows prevented me from an unobstructed view, but I felt I could see my target well enough to take a decent shot. I tried to calm my breathing so as to hold my rifle steady. POW! The sheep lifted their heads and began to walk up the valley floor. POW! I took a second shot at a little over 150 yards. Now the sheep increased their pace to a trot. I jumped up and began running up the valley on the side hill. At the next large boulder pile, I took another quick shot at probably 225 yards. No ram down, and they were getting further away from me even though I kept running on the hillside, trying to keep up. I had only eight shells with me and I expended the remaining five as the sheep moved further and further away from me. The last shot was at least 500 yards at a moving target, with very little chance of bringing down my World Record Ram.

With no more ammo, a pounding heart, and thoroughly exhausted from running on the hillside at an altitude of 6,000 feet, I leaned against a large boulder and cried; the chance of a lifetime blown. The sheep were now maybe 600 yards ahead of me and climbing slightly above me. They slowed to a walk, stopped, and began to graze. I couldn't believe that the scare I just gave them wasn't sufficient to drive them out of sight and over into the next valley. It was as if they were shouting back to me, "You didn't scare us, you're a lousy shot, and we know you are out of shells. Dry your tears and go home. See you next year— maybe."

I watched them for 10 or 15 minutes, knowing that there was nothing more that I could do to bring that ram home. I turned, and very dejectedly began my descent to the valley floor, and back to where I had left Tom. He had witnessed my whole effort and offered some consoling words as we met. We returned, in silence, to the cabin. At dinner we went over my effort to get a shot at the big ram. It was obvious that, right from the start, having to begin my stalk across the valley floor with no cover put me at a great disadvantage. Then there was no way for me to know that I would not be able to see Tom's hand signals in the shadow of the willows. He said that as I was climbing up the little gully the sheep were moving down to their watering hole. This, and my inexperience of shooting downhill at a steep angle, were the back breakers. I have since read that in either case of shooting targets above or below your position, you should aim high. There are mathematical formulas of figuring how high or low to aim, but I could only guess and, I guessed wrong. When I discovered the sheep were below me, I felt I had only two options, either move back down the gully or take a shot from where I was. There was a third option—just waiting to see what the sheep did. That option did not come to my mind. Even now, some 40 years later, I still have intense emotional feelings when I think about the hunt and my missing out on a "once-in-a-lifetime" chance to add a record Dall ram to my wall. I'd like to say: "C'est la vie," but it's too painful to joke about; 10 times worse than when Ohio State beats Michigan in football. Ecclesiastes 3:6 tells us that there is "a time to gain and a time to lose." It's hard to lose.

NOMEITES

This is not a hunting or fishing story per se. I practiced orthodontics in Nome for 43 years and feel I would be remiss if I did not comment on the special people and happenings in Nome during this time of my life. Nome is an old gold rush town on the Bering Sea coast. In 1898 the "Three Lucky Swedes" discovered gold in Anvil Creek and that started a stampede to Nome; or, as we say, "Nome, by golly!" The town of Nome was founded in 1901 when there were 10,000 miners, merchants, Natives, hustlers, hookers, horses, dogs, inebriates, and a few renegades, all crowded together because of gold and greed. A very colorful place—the Last Frontier, full of "Mother Lode" hope, tears, bankruptcy, and tragedy.

In 1971, Ray and Carla Lang came to my office in Anchorage and asked me if I was interested in coming to Nome to practice orthodontics? Ray had graduated from DePaul Dental School in Chicago, after which he accepted a dental assignment with the U.S. Public Health Service in Bethel, Alaska. Now he was in private practice in Nome. My "yes" to their question, was the beginning of a great friendship as well as the adventure of practicing orthodontics throughout Alaska. Over the next 43 years, I provided orthodontic care in Anchorage, Fairbanks, Nome, Adak Naval Air Station, Sand Point, Wasilla, Palmer, Dillingham, Cordova, a kitchen in Kotzebue, and a cabin on the Karluk River on Kodiak Island. Usually, one or two members of my Anchorage staff and I packed our ortho goodies in suitcases on a Friday, caught an Alaska Air flight to wherever, worked Saturday, often Sunday, and flew home Sunday evening. We did this hundreds of times over the 43 years. Except for Anchorage and Cordova, we were the first to offer orthodontic care in these towns and villages.

As I mentioned, Ray was a Chicago boy who wound up in the remote Alaska Native village of Bethel. He was badly injured on a Polar Bear hunt, and wound up as a patient in the Bethel hospital in which he worked. Not to worry, this was one of the best things that ever happened to him. His nurse just happened to be Carla! Romance, marriage, children, and dentistry in Nome, ensued. It was a script right out of Hollywood. It had to be, you see, because Carla's father was a Hollywood stunt man until age pushed him into being a Hollywood photographer.

It took a very special woman to handle Ray. Let me say, with great affection, Raymond's character could be described, conservatively, as intelligent, hardworking, great sense of humor, fearless, and strongly cantankerous. I watched these two interact over 40 years, and Carla fit the bill perfectly. Oh yes, there were times of "walking on eggs," but the evidence of strong love was always there.

Ray Lang's dental partner was Dan Stang, a Wisconsin Badger who graduated from Marquette Dental School. Dan had hunting, fishing, and trapping in his blood stream. He and Ray built a very comfortable cabin on the Niukluk (nee uk luck) River, at Council, some 60 miles from Nome. Ray took me hunting, fishing, and recreational flying in his PA-14 Piper Cub. Many people had dog teams in Nome, and Ray and Carla each had teams. Ray entered and won many local weekend dog races and ran the Iditarod once.

Council was another gold rush town with a population of 10,000 in the early 1900s. There are a few original buildings, in varying states of decay, still left. Along the gravel road from Nome to Council there are a few old gold mining areas, with the remains of gold dredges, and a rusting narrow-gauge train—echoes of the long-past Nome Gold Rush. Council is now a recreational destination for Nomeites who have built summer cabins along the river. Dan spends almost every weekend and much of every summer at his cabin in Council. He drives out on the gravel road or travels by snow machine. Several stories come to mind when I think back over the many years I worked in Nome, one relating to a moose hunt and the other had roots in Washington D.C.

Lifetime friend, Ray Lang, Nome dentist, and his dog team out for a run.
Photo credit: Carla Lang.

NIUKLUK MOOSE

Even though the climate is very harsh during Nome winters, and the terrain is mostly vast tundra, there is a reasonable moose population. Tundra is primarily an area that is treeless and covered with Reindeer moss, lichens, blueberry bushes, and low bush cranberries. The Nomeites harvest moose mostly along the limited roads to Council and the village of Teller. The Niukluk River and the White River allow those with boats to hunt more distant areas. A few hunters are fortunate enough to own planes and can land on river bars in remote locations where the odds of getting a moose are much greater.

Ray and Dan invited me and some of Dan's Wisconsin relatives to go moose hunting in the Council area. Strum, Dan's Eskimo friend and dental assistant, also joined our party. We drove to Council in pickups loaded with our hunting gear and food. Dan's cabin was across the river, so we had to ford the river in the trucks. Ray flew out in his PA-14.

The next morning, Holly, Dan's friend, a retired rough and tumble Marine Corps sergeant, joined us. Holly and Dan had 18-foot river boats, with 75 hp jet unit motors. These were necessary for travel where the Niukluk River was shallow. At Council, it's about 30 yards wide, and flows at least 5 knots.

Above Council the trees are primarily willows which are the main food source for moose. Below Council, there are Willow, Spruce, and Cottonwood trees along the bank. We were going to hunt 20 or 25 miles upriver, so it was decided to set up a tent camp about 15 miles above Council.

Ray took off in his Cub to scout out the area we wanted to hunt. He and Dan had agreed to a long river bar where he could land and we could camp. By midday we had our camp set up and decided to hunt the area around camp. We saw plenty of moose signs, but no moose. Our consolation prize was picking Alaska's tasty wild blueberries. When Ray returned, he said he saw several moose a few miles upstream. This was encouraging news. Tomorrow we would get serious about our hunt.

The next morning was heavy with frost and made for a quick exit from a warm sleeping bag to get dressed. Breakfast was strong coffee, eggs, and pancakes—all thanks to our trusty Coleman stoves. The day was going to be another fall football day … temperature around 50 degrees, no wind, and not a cloud in the sky. We headed up stream for about 10 miles to where Ray had seen several moose. The willows were thick here, and they reached at least 12 feet high—making a long shot difficult except when close to the river. We divided up into three teams, agreed to be back at the boats within three hours, and headed into the thick willows hoping to spook out a decent bull. I could see that this was not going to be an easy hunt, and my hopes were not high. We poked around in and out of patches of willows and along a couple of small streams. There were plenty of moose tracks, and we could see where they had been browsing on the Willows, but there were none to shoot at.

Ray and I were the first group to return to the boat, followed by Dan and his Wisconsin relatives. We were standing around, figuratively, "Shooting the Bull," and chatting about our lack of luck, when suddenly a real bull stepped out of the willows about a hundred yards up river. Dan quickly said, "Dick, take your shot. Take your shot." I quickly brought my trusty 7mm up and held the cross hairs of my scope on the bull's shoulder. POW. He went down but immediately got up and began to walk out into the river. A chorus of voices said, "Take another shot!" Just great. I'm repeating the scene of a moose kill years ago on the Chilkoot River near Haines. The end result was the same. Four of us couldn't pull the moose into shallower water so we had to gut and butcher him out in the river. The only fun part this time was that the grayling in the river began to swim right between our legs to feed on any butchering scraps that floated away. We loaded up Holly's boat with moose meat, and he headed back to Council to put it in a freezer.

That night, the camp was filled with tall tales—the joy of success and a few shots from a bottle of Peppermint Schnapps in which Strum had also dropped some blueberries. We all headed to our tents for a well-deserved sleep. Suddenly, an uproar ensued from Dan's cousin's tent. A few oaths and unprintable words came forth … and out flew a butchered moose head. Strum was a trickster. He had slid the moose head into the sleeping bag of one of Dan's cousins who didn't appreciate the joke; but he was outnumbered with everyone's laughter.

Niukluk moose.

Niukluk grayling.

IDITAROD LASAGNA

My Nome policy for my staff was to give them their Alaska Air award miles, pay them a dollar more an hour, and cook them a gourmet meal. They all loved going to Nome. Not only for the benefits, but we always had a good time staying at the Lang's.

Let me take a brief Iditarod Race detour. The famous Iditarod dog sled race, of about 1000 miles, begins with a ceremonial start in Anchorage on the first Saturday in March. The real race begins Sunday in Willow, a small community 70 miles north of Anchorage.

The first Iditarod Race was held in 1973. It is a memorial race to commemorate the 1925 dog team run from Nenana to Nome to deliver lifesaving serum during a diphtheria epidemic. Twenty mushers and about 150 sled dogs, transported the diphtheria antitoxin over the 674 miles from Nenana to Nome. They accomplished this in dog sled relay teams in 5½ days. The weather was stormy with temperatures down to more than 60 degrees below zero and wind chill factors of 85 degrees below zero. Mushers suffered severe frostbite and several dogs died. This effort saved Nome and the surrounding small communities from a developing epidemic of diphtheria.

The early Iditarod races took as long as a month. Now, because of faster dogs, better equipment, and improved musher skill, that has been reduced to 8 or 9 days. As many as 87 mushers, men and women from all over the world, start out in Anchorage, driving teams of 12 to 16 dogs. It's required that they finish with at least five of their original dogs. They follow the Iditarod trail across frozen tundra, mountains, and rivers to reach the Bering Sea coast at Unalakleet. From there they travel up the coast to Nome. The winner gets as much as $50,000 and a Dodge pickup truck.

On three occasions we planned our Nome orthodontic trip to coincide with the time we thought the winner of the Iditarod Race would arrive. The town siren goes off as the racer approaches the city limits … and, for the winner, a large crowd gathers to cheer the victor across the finish line. It might be 3 a.m., 30 below zero, and blowing, but you have to haul yourself out of a warm bed and hustle down to Main Street. It's always a heroic feat to come across the finish line first. Both men and women have won the race.

One evening, at sunset, I drove out about five miles along the Bering Sea coast towards Safety—the last check point about twenty miles from Nome. A lone musher and his team, out on the ice, were slowly crossing my view of the setting sun, leaving their shadows extending towards me. I was overwhelmed with emotion as I tried to peer into the musher's mind and thoughts. I imagined the recalling of the thousand grueling miles now behind … the blizzards, sub-zero temperatures, caring for the dogs, little sleep, fighting fatigue, and now the end is near. Volunteers will care for the dogs; hugs, cheers, and tears from family and friends, a hot meal, a shower, a warm bed, and a night of uninterrupted sleep lie ahead. No matter what place you're in … First or last—winner or holder of the Red Lantern, last place, it's a great personal achievement and victory. In the Acrtic silence, I just stood there, overwhelmed with emotion, holding back the tears, and watched the musher and team grow smaller … and smaller … as they approached the finish line in Nome. God bless you musher and team, well done, well done! "You have fought the good fight, you have finished the race, you have kept the faith" (2 Timothy 4:7).

Since Ray and Carla were so connected to the dog racing community, their house was a mecca for visiting Iditarod-people. Ray posted a sign on the front door, "Swenson: enter through back door only!" Rick Swenson was a multiple Iditarod champion, and Ray was always ready to keep him humble. The coffee pot was always on, and people were coming and going all hours of the day and night. There were people sleeping in every bed, on the floor, on every couch, and even in the bath tub. All conversation centered around dog teams, dog trading, dog feeding, dog breeding, lead dogs, race strategy … dogs, dogs, dogs!!!

During one particular Iditarod Race, I decided to cook lasagna. I had never prepared this dish and thought it would be quick and easy. I got Sali's recipe and headed for Carrs grocery store in Anchorage to purchase the rest of my dinner items. The lasagna noodle box had its own recipe so I sort of combined it with Sali's. That night, after seeing patients all day, I began putting my dinner together. There were at least 10 at the table: Ray, Carla, my staff, a short balding guy with a full beard, and three others I did not know. My dinner guests were just chatting, laughing, and having a glass of wine, all expectant for a taste of my fine cuisine. I'm humming away in Carla's small, but efficient kitchen; all is well in "Nome, by golly."

I served my "killer" salad with maple syrup dressing that everyone loves. Next, and right on time, I pulled the "cooked to perfection" lasagna out of the oven and served everyone a generous piece. Soon the conversation at the table stopped; everyone looked at me in silence. Then the short guy with the balding head and full beard said, "Richard, you forgot to cook the noodles first." I was confused and crushed. My lasagna was bone dry. I mistakenly did not cook the noodles ahead of time. The dry noodles I used sucked all the moisture out of the lasagna.

Scripture clearly tells us in Romans 5:3-4, that God builds character in us through suffering. Well, my character jumped at least two notches or maybe 10 that night. It turned out that the short balding guy with a full beard was Gerome—who had been a White House chef for President George H. W. Bush. Having such a knowledgeable, and almost famous, guest at my dinner table was highly unusual and his gentle criticism was almost a compliment. You agree, of course? No one starved, no one got sick, and actually their laughter outweighed any complaint. I think we all went through two pounds of butter to help the tasty, but dry lasagna, slide down.

COOK'S REDEMPTION

A few years later, we were again in Nome with the hope of seeing the Iditarod winner come across the finish line. After work on Friday, we headed for the Lang's. As expected, the house was full of Iditarod -connected people. I noticed that Gerome was there and remembered my painful lasagna flop of several years earlier. I quickly asked Carla if I could bag off of cooking dinner that night. Fortunately, Gerome had brought along a turkey and had planned to cook dinner. As you might expect, we had an excellent dinner. Carla implied that we could have leftovers the next night, so I thought I was off the hook.

Saturday evening rolled around, and I guess the leftovers were eaten by all the Iditarod guests. I was requested to prepare my pork tenderloin and cherry sauce for dinner. Okay, I thought, nothing ventured, nothing gained. I set about, with some trepidation, to prepare a dinner for the President's chef. I served up the pork tenderloin and cherry sauce and everyone seemed happy and satisfied. After dinner Gerome came over to me, put his hand on my shoulder, and said: "Richard, that was a very good sauce." Redemption felt so good.

A REAL DUESY

I will tell one last Nome story. As I mentioned before, Carla's father was a Hollywood stuntman who transitioned to becoming a photographer. On the walls of the Lang's home were many large black and white photographs of Hollywood stars: Wallace Berry, Dennis Morgan, and Randolph Scott, are a few I remember. The photographs were taken by Carla's father on movie sets. Some of the movies I had seen as a child. There was a small photograph on Carla's kitchen wall that I had noticed many times. It was a scene in mountainous country of a long four-door convertible car with the top down. There is camping gear tied to the sides and back of the car. A small dog is just behind a mule deer that is strapped to one of the long sweeping fenders. There are three hunters in the car. One of the men has on a leather helmet-like hat—the kind pilots wore in open-cockpit airplanes. I had one as a kid with goggles and a chin strap. It was one of my prized possessions. Carla had told me that the picture was taken during one of her father's hunting trips.

On one of our Nome trips, Carla's mother, Mrs. Saugstad, was visiting, and was there for our evening meal. I had a hunch about the car in the photograph, and I hoped Carla's mother could settle my curiosity. Our conversation about the photograph went something like this: "Mrs. Saugstad, do you know anything about this photo?"

"Yes, it's a picture of my husband, my father, and a friend hunting in the High Sierras."

Then I asked, "And do you know anything about the car in the picture? Do you know what kind of car it is? Do you know how much you could sell it for today?"

She replied, "I do know that it was a Duesenberg, but that's about it."

"Well, Mrs. Saugstad, yes, that car is a Duesenberg convertible. Today, restored, it would be worth at least $250,000!"

Her reply was, "I see. Well, Richard, that's not the whole story. You see, we had two of those cars … two Duesenbergs. One of them had transmission problems. It sat next to the house for many years and was used for parts. Eventually, both Duesenbergs were sitting in the yard, rusting away. When my husband was off working on a movie set … the junkman came by and offered me $100 for both of them. I was glad to get rid of those eyesores. My marriage … well … my marriage was never quite the same after that." That, I could well imagine.

A real Duesy in the high Sierras.
Photo credit: Carla Lang.

PART V

LOST

COVENANT BROKEN

In 1982, after 23 years, our marriage covenant was broken. Sali and I were divorced. Scripture describes marriage as, "'The two shall become one flesh'" (Matthew 19:5). The truth of this statement becomes clearly evident in a divorce, because it is a painful tearing apart of the flesh, as well as the bonds of marriage. When I consider all the reasons for seeking a divorce, the only conclusion I can reach is … it's ultimately a selfish act—one of, "I want this. I demand that." The romance and love of our initial relationship had turned into disappointments and dissatisfaction … life's trials and tribulations had beaten us down. Our spiritual enemy, Satan, had gained the upper hand. The tender moments of "I love you, and I need you" are gone. Peanut butter and jelly sandwiches were now filled with sawdust. There was no more … "This is the day that the Lord has made; we will rejoice and be glad in it." (Psalms 118:24). Anger and tears and broken dreams were scattered about on the floor, and we weren't able to hire "Merry Maids" to clean up the mess. We had burned through several marriage counselors who offered no acceptable wisdom or solution. Attorneys and accountants were hired … time and money was wasted. Painful emotions came forth, uninvited … and life was like hell.

Amidst unresolved questions about what is Truth?… and what is Fair?… and where is God in all this?... the divorce was granted. There was some emotional relief, but doubts and pain still remained. It was ultimately not a happy day—a day we would honestly celebrate. Life goes on, and we have to pick up the pieces and live in the present.

I remember quoting to myself from the Declaration of Independence: "We hold these truths to be self-evident, that all men are created equal, that they are endowed by their Creator with certain unalienable Rights, that among these are Life, Liberty, and the pursuit of Happiness." It was time for me to pursue Life, Liberty, and Happiness. How nice, how selfish, and how overly optimistic. How detached from reality. It took me years to figure that truth out.

As Sali and I went our separate ways, I soon realized that every family celebration was compromised … every birthday, every

Christmas and Thanksgiving, every graduation ceremony, and every birth of grandchildren. There was always an awkwardness and tension, like a cloud hovering over what should have been a joyful time. This bothered me a great deal. I wondered if this would remain the same for a lifetime.

We still continued to attend a church. We still heard the Gospel message, still read our Bibles, and went to Bible studies. The one Scripture that continually seemed to speak to me was in the book of Malachi. In the second chapter of Malachi (my paraphrase from *The Message*), we read, in verses 10-16, "Do we not all have one God, one Father, and one Creator? Then why do we treat each other so treacherously? Why do we profane the covenant of our Father that binds us together? God was there when you spoke your marriage vows to your young bride. Now you've broken the faith-bond with your covenant wife. God, not you, made marriage. His Spirit inhabits even the smallest details of marriage. God expects us to guard the spirit of our marriage. Furthermore, God has declared, 'I hate divorce.'" This Scripture came to my mind almost every day. It imparted a serious guilt feeling, a feeling that I was failing God, failing Sali, failing my family, and failing my friends.

I, as a Christian, wasn't putting God first in my life. I was putting "self" above all—my wants, my pleasures, my desires. The end result was that I was not living a life that glorified God.

DROWNING IN CHANNEL 7

About six months before our divorce, on a beautiful spring Sunday morning in 1982, I was walking down the aisle in church, "a safe place to be," when I received a tap on my shoulder. I turned around to be greeted by a man named Mike Parker. He introduced himself and asked me, "Can we talk after church?" and I replied, "Yes, we can."

Following the church service Mr. Parker informed me that he was getting together a group of investors to apply for a television station license. He said there were only two licenses available in the whole

United States, and one of them was here, in Anchorage. Further, he planned to have Christian programs as a part of their regular format. I told him that I was definitely interested. The initial investment was $13,000 from each of the 13 investors, four from the Anchorage area, and nine from the Seattle-Tacoma area.

It didn't take Mike Parker long to assemble 13 investors, him being the 13th one. Our first investors meeting was in Seattle. We went through the formalities of introducing ourselves, agreeing that Mike should lead the way, and each investor was to chip in $13,000. An attorney had to be hired, and an application for the television station license made. Everyone was excited about this investment adventure, and I know we all had "Visions of sugar plumbs dancing in our heads—Dreams of fortunes to be made!"

In a conversation with a woman Mike had brought to our meeting as secretary, I learned a bit of Mike's history. She informed me that he had been the mayor of Tacoma and had also been the youngest legislator in the Washington State House of Representatives. I did not inquire about Mike's investment history or experience. This was a very big mistake, which I, and all the investors, came to regret.

As I recall, we all had to fill out a sort of lengthy biography-character form that the Federal Communications Commission required. I didn't know what the odds of our acquiring the license were, but within two or three months we were awarded the television station license. We now owned the rights to Channel 7 in Anchorage, Alaska. It eventually became KTBY Channel 4.

With our license in hand, we secured a $2.5 million-dollar loan from a local bank. Then began all the work of securing office space, hiring a general manager and a program director, finding an experienced television engineer, hiring office personnel, and sales people. Mike was responsible for most of these tasks. The engineer purchased and supervised the installation of all the necessary equipment, and he and Mike negotiated for the very critical antenna location. This took the better part of a year. During this time, we had several investor meetings, some in Anchorage and some in Seattle or Tacoma. Mike expressed the need for each investor to chip in another $5000. There was a bit of grumbling, but I think everyone complied.

It was an exciting night when we had our gala "ON the Air" reception in our station offices in the Bradley Building. The mayor was there, most of the investors, a few local and state political leaders, and a number of other invited guests. There were a few speeches, a ribbon cutting ceremony, some very good hors d'oeurvres, and moderately priced wine. After a year and a half—our dream was about to come true. At last we were on the air as Anchorage's fourth or fifth television station. Now the return on the investment would begin to flow in. Time for me to place my order for a Mercedes and a Cessna 185 airplane on floats, so I could join my other dental peers flying around Alaska to hunt and fish.

I guess that we, like any fledgling business, struggled in the beginning. Our sales force was working hard, beating the bushes, to secure advertisers. The advertising revenue was critical to our success, and we had plenty of competitors seeking the same dollars. Another unforeseen factor, critical to our success, was our television signal. The highest building in Anchorage at that time was the 22-story Westward Hotel, now the Hilton Hotel. We tried to secure a spot on their roof, but other stations had already secured this prime location and objected to our joining them. I'm not sure where our engineer found a location for our antenna, but our signal was marginal. This was a serious negative for our sales force when it came to selling advertising for a station with a picture that was not of the highest quality.

We stumbled along for almost a year and reached the point where we were losing almost $30,000 to $40,000 a month. The possibility of bankruptcy was looming ahead, and the investors began to bail out. It was time to sell the station. We had creditors by the dozen, all threatening us. Our beautiful dream was falling apart. There goes my Mercedes and the Cessna 185 on floats.

Mike put the station up for sale; our asking price was $2.5 million. We had a very strong response from potential buyers showing interest in the station. They came to Anchorage to check out the station and the revenue numbers, then sort of move to the sidelines without making an offer. They were like wolves circling a fire in the dark, waiting for the fire embers to die out, then grab the prey. In other words, if we had to cease broadcasting and our signal went dark, a fire sale would result. The buyer could get the station for pennies on the dollar and we would have no money to pay our creditors. I could see bankruptcy and lawsuits in the future.

For reasons unknown to me, I seemed to be the only investor who checked on the buyer possibilities with Mike, and went over to the station to ask the manager how things were going. I was highly concerned about our failing situation. I also was calling out to God for a solution, one that I could not see … a Miracle—that only He could provide. I didn't have $30,000 or $40,000 a month to keep the station going.

I was living in a small condominium complex. I had a brass bed, and when I was trying to go to sleep, my heart beat, from the stress I was under, was so strong—that it shook the bed just enough to make it squeak. The squeak, of course, kept me from sleeping. I said to myself, *This is crazy, my own heart beat is keeping me awake!*

Now, I know some of you, my readers, do not believe in God, do not serve Him, and are not concerned about the consequences of not having your sins forgiven. Some, a rare few, have no concept of sin. You have no concern about a promise of Eternal Life after death. You assume that, after death, your soul and spirit just fall into a dark void, tumbling and falling, tumbling and falling, forever, or after death it's just some sort of empty nothingness, a hell of your own design. I think your unbelief is due to a lack of information about God, about His character, about how much He loves you, and about His plan for your life and your salvation. I beg of you NOT to live on in ignorance. Seek out a Christian Believer who can help you get educated about the living God, Who loves you, and seeks to take you under His wings, to redeem you, to enable you to stand before Him, a <u>forgiven person</u>, and receive the Gift of Eternal Life in heaven with Him.

With that said, it's another Sunday morning, I'm not in church where I should be, but home in my bachelor pad, my condo. This Sunday a tap comes, not on my shoulder, but on my door. It's my neighbor, Ron Bradley, who also happens to be our station's landlord, and we are deeply in debt to him for unpaid rent. Ron says, "Richard, come over and talk to me."

A few hours later I went next door to the Bradley's. I spent two hours with Ron and his wife, Peggy. During that time Ron told me that Mike Parker was highly disliked by the Seattle-Tacoma bankers. They had had other failed investment dealings with him and many people had lost thousands of dollars, some their entire retirement funds, due to Mike's poor management. They had no complementary words for Mike Parker. They preferred that he be in jail.

Then Ron told me everything that was wrong with our station and especially with our leadership. He was fully aware of our financial crisis and the lack of any offers to buy the station. You can imagine how low and defeated I felt, now knowing what a failure this investment was becoming. Ron, quietly looked over at me and said, "I'll buy the station."

Don't tell me there isn't a God who loves His children. A God, when we earnestly, in strong faith, call out to Him, will hear our prayers and answer. Ron's miracle offer was 1.95 million dollars for the station. We could handle the remaining debt owed to the bank. I needed to learn the lesson in Romans 12:12: "Rejoice in hope, be patient in tribulation, be constant in prayer" (ESV).

I went home rejoicing, leaping for joy. A tremendous weight had been lifted from my shoulders. The bankruptcy worries were gone and my heartbeat returned to normal. My bed would not squeak tonight! I could sleep peacefully again. "Thank you, Lord. Thank you Lord!" was all I could say, until I fell asleep.

THE LAST SHEEP HUNT

In 1983, a couple of guys from Abbot Loop church were going on a sheep hunt in the Wrangell Mountains. Jim Brenn and Jim Anderson had hunted the Hawkins Glacier area the previous year and wanted to hunt there again. They invited me and Chuck Gold to go along. Having reached my 50th birthday, I did have some concerns about being strong enough to climb around in the mountains. I had a strong hunch that this was going to be my last sheep hunt.

Two weeks later, on a beautiful day in August, we loaded our gear into a twin-engine Aero Commander that the church owned. Our pilot, Dick Crow, flew us to McCarthy—a small village a couple of miles from the famous Kennecott Mine that I mentioned earlier, on my first sheep hunt.

In McCarthy, we were met by our guide, Tom Spurnak. Tom and his wife lived nearby in a beautiful log cabin on the banks of a crystal clear stream. We were flown, one at a time, in Tom's Interstate (similar to a Super Cub), to his cabin. Tom's wife prepared a delicious dinner for us, and we spent the night there. The next day, Tom flew us one at a time, to his Hawkins Glacier airstrip. He had placed 50 gallon blue barrels on each side of the airstrip just far enough apart to clear his wing tips. This made the landings a bit dicey, but Tom told us it kept most pilots off his strip. There also was a small cabin at the strip that came in handy if the weather soured.

We arranged with Tom to do an airdrop of our food, fuel, stove, and some gear. Tom knew exactly where our camp was going to be, since Brenn and Anderson had hunted with him the year before. There was an alder-covered slope just behind the tent area where he would drop the boxes. He was to come in low, and slow, and push the boxes out so they fell into the alders. This broke their fall, caused minimal damage, and made them easy to retrieve. Now it was time to "Load'em up and move out," a command I heard a thousand times in the U.S. Army. We shouldered our back packs and bid farewell to Tom.

This was a new area for me to hunt, so I didn't know what the trail was like. As at Eagle Creek, we were in for another six-mile hike at a pace of one mile an hour. The trail was basically flat, and followed along the edge of Hawkins Glacier's lateral moraine—a glacial tongue that creeps from the face of the glacier to its melting point at a river, lake, or tidewater. It's made up of ice, rocks, and dirt. The primary difficulty on such a trail is that we have to walk on small boulders and football sized rocks that beat our ankles to death. If there were six paces on flat ground we were thankful. After a couple miles, I began to dread the return hike with a heavier pack—hopefully, with a sheep horn and salted cape on my back. It was a crystal-clear day, not a cloud in the sky, probably in the 60s. A good day to sweat out the "bad humors."

The last mile of our trek, we moved away from the moraine, to hike up the middle of a mile-wide, rock-strewn, ancient glacial river bed. Our camp site was on the edge of this river bed in a stand of tall willows. While we were setting up our tents, we heard the sound of an approaching aircraft. It was Tom Spurnak's Interstate approaching, but his altitude was at least 2000 feet instead of 200. Perhaps we were wrong, and this was some other plane. The four of us stood watching as a box tumbled out of the plane. Down, down, it came, and exploded as it hit the rocky surface of the river bed. There were a few expletives expressed as we watched the plane turn and fly out of sight over the glacier. Jim Brenn took off to retrieve whatever was left of the contents. We now kept our gaze out over the glacier. About 10 minutes later, at a lower altitude, we spotted Tom's plane. Well before he reached us, another box with its trailing orange surveyor tape, fell out of sight to the glacial surface.

I scooted up the hill behind our camp so I could see where the next box was going to hit. I stood beside a car-sized boulder that had a flat surface aimed toward the plane's flight. The lower edge of the boulder was knife sharp, straight, and parallel to the ground. Beneath it was a dug-out area that easily could accommodate a large bear in hibernation. I leaned against the rock … watching, as Tom approached at maybe 300 feet. Out came the next box—too high for the alders, and headed right for me. I dove uphill as it smacked the rock's edge, tore apart, and plowed into the dugout below. The next 20 minutes I spent trying to sort out and save the box's contents. The paper towels were okay, some canned goods were badly dented, the butter was okay, but the jars of peanut butter and jam were a gooey mess mixed together with glass and dirt—totally a scrambled loss.

I carried the salvageable items to the camp site. Jim Brenn returned with what he could salvage from the river bed box. A lengthy discussion ensued as we tried to sort out just what had happened and take inventory of our situation. Our cooking stove and fuel were apparently in the box that fell out over the glacier—unretrievable! The peanut butter and jam, bread, and other items were missing or destroyed. Dinner was a meager offering of odds and ends.

The next morning, Jim Brenn decided to cook us pancakes in the one frying pan that survived. This turned out to be rather humorous. The first bite we took of the pancakes revealed that the Bisquick and the dish soap, which were in the river bed box he had retrieved, had gotten mixed together. Jim admitted that he had tried to separate, and save, both the Bisquick and soap flakes. Thanks Jimmy, but no thanks.

We could not spend another five days hunting with the food we had left. Everyone was disgusted with Tom's disastrous airdrop and many questions were unanswered. Jim Anderson and Chuck volunteered to hike all the way back to the air strip, hoping Tom was there, and hoping he could replace all of our lost supplies. This was a big gamble, and could turn out to be a long difficult hike for nothing. Jim Brenn and I bid them farewell, not wanting to see our whole hunt wasted and hoping and praying for the best.

The next day, around noon, Jim and Chuck returned … with full packs and in good spirits. They told us this almost unbelievable story. During their long hike out, they discussed how they should approach Tom. Basically, give him both barrels, and demand that he resolve our predicament—for which he was responsible! When they were approaching Tom's airstrip, they could see him walking toward them. Tom raised his hand and yelled to them, "Stop! … I think you have something to say to me!" The laughter that followed drained all the anger and frustration out of Jim and Chuck. Tom was well aware of our situation, and with our grocery and supply list, he flew off to secure the items we needed. While he was gone, Jim and Chuck checked out the small cabin area. From the empty booze bottles lying around, it was evident that Tom was probably an alcoholic, and used this private and remote cabin to indulge in his bad habit. We concluded that he was obviously drunk when he made our air drop. I became very concerned, since we had to rely on Spurnak Air to fly us out on our return home. I had the comforting thought, sober or drunk, he still had the ability to land between the blue barrels. Tom returned with every item we requested and as an added bonus his wife sent along a loaf of her homemade bread. We were well-fed for the rest of our hunt.

Chuck and I were to hunt together. The next morning, we headed across the river bed and climbed a mountain south of the camp. We spent the day scoping out possible areas where the sheep might be. While scoping I looked down at the ground and saw small delicate flowers in bloom. I knew that at an altitude of 7000 feet, there was only about a 90-day window of above freezing temperatures, and maybe four months of no snow. God's Creation is amazing. We spent the whole day walking where probably no one else had ever walked. We were skunked. No sheep, but all in all … a beautiful day in the magnificent Alaskan mountains … God's Country.

The weather remained clear and warm … especially for August. We then decided to traverse the Hawkins Glacier moraine and climb a mountain to the north. I had never ventured out onto a field of melting ice before. From a distance it seemed to be a stationary and silent river of ice, but when we got out on it; we discovered it's a living thing. The melting ice creates noisy, rushing streams. Also, the moraine surface was covered by rocks and gravel that noisily, continually rolled down into the streams. They, in turn, flowed down into ice funnels that had no bottom. The streams of water just disappeared. We had to constantly watch each step so as not to slip and slide down into one of those giant ice funnels to disappear from sight forever. I never had any idea of the danger out there. It took us over an hour to pick our way across the mile-wide moraine.

Then, Chuck and I separated to climb and hunt different areas. I chose a steep chute to explore. A light pack and my 7mm made it easy to move along. The odds were again that this area had never been hunted, or at least, very infrequently. I headed up the chute higher and higher ... foolishly, alone. The chute kept getting steeper and steeper. Then, I reached a point where I could not turn around and go back down without falling. As usual, when I am in such dire straits, I begin to seriously pray. I especially prayed that I was near the chute ridge top. I hugged the mountain surface and pulled myself along another 10 or 20 yards—finally reaching a narrow ridgetop sheep trail. The strong odor of fresh sheep droppings was a new but welcome smell to me.

After a breather, I crawled on hands and knees to reach a safer place so I could stand and look around. I had never been in such a "sheepy" place. There were many well-worn trails, with sheep hair snagged on sharp rock edges, sheep hoof tracks, and piles of smelly sheep droppings. I scoped out the area but saw no sheep. With all the sign about, I had every expectation to take a ram from this area. I poked along on this high trail for about a half mile but didn't see a thing. I had left Chuck about three hours ago, and now I had to find a way down to the glacial moraine and return to our camp. The steepness of the mountainside slopes became more favorable, and I found a trail that led me down to and along the glacier moraine. It was my good fortune to find Chuck coming towards me on the same trail. We exchanged hunting stories, and neither of us were successful that day. I wasn't looking forward to crossing the moraine again, but we had no choice. It was already late in the day as we began our slow journey back across the moraine to camp.

I should mention an odd event that happened on this hunt. One afternoon, we all happened to be in camp. We were out of sight because of the tall willows that grew in this area. Suddenly, we heard the sound of an approaching aircraft—a yellow super cub appeared and was soon followed by two others. They circled and landed out on the river bed, probably 600 yards from us. We watched as the pilots got out of their planes, had some conversation, then got back in their planes and took off.

We are out in the middle of nowhere and this strange event happened. Our camp analysis was—these guys must have been dealing in drugs and thought that this area was a safe place to rendezvous. We all could have taken aim and shot out their tires—thus, spoiling their day. Of course, this would have complicated our hunting trip and created other problems, so best to stay hidden from the criminals.

Our last day was now upon us, and no one had taken a ram. This was such a good area, with plenty of sign, so we could not understand why none of us hadn't even seen any ewes and lambs. Chuck wanted to take a look at an area high above our camp. It was going to be a hard climb, but by now I was in reasonable shape and felt up to it. We headed east up the edge of the river bed and began to climb up behind the camp site. I'd say we climbed for two or three hours and reached an elevation of 7500 feet. This was higher than I had ever hunted before. We reached an ice field that we had to cross, and thankfully, we had packed our crampons.

The valley we wanted to look into was across the ice field about 300 yards ahead of us. Another warm, cloudless day, with no cover … reminding me of a previous sheep hunt. The spot where we were headed was going to be above where we thought we might find sheep which was to our advantage. We slowly approached the edge of the ice field. Our view was of an almost vertical rock wall that ended in the valley floor, some 200 feet below us. Across the valley, and lying on a ledge below us, we spotted two legal rams enjoying the warm sunshine. One couldn't ask for a more perfect shot at about 100 yards. We decided which ram each of us should take, got into position, and on the count of three took our shots! It took only one shot. My ram barely moved, but Chuck's took one leap and fell a long way to the valley floor.

There was no easy way we could reach our rams. We had to hike back across the ice field, past camp, and finally up the valley that led to where Chuck's ram lay. When we got to Chuck's ram, we found that it had hit so hard on the rocks below, that one horn had been knocked completely off. With some difficulty, we retrieved my ram from the ledge above us. By the time we got the horns, the cape, and the meat packed and ready to head back to camp we had only about an hour and a half of daylight left. My pack must have weighed 80 pounds and Chuck's was at least 100 pounds. Fortunately, it was a downhill pack, but after a half hour, I could no longer carry such a heavy load. It

felt like I was going to blow out my hip sockets. We decided to carry the horns, the cape, and whatever meat that would make a reasonable load. The remaining meat was stashed away to be retrieved tomorrow; that is, of course, if a bear didn't beat us to it. Happily, we strode into camp, and then began the stories; the joshing, sprinkled with a little obligatory stretching of the truth. Our trip home with Spurnak Air was safe, sober, and uneventful. And yes, this was my last sheep hunt.

With Chuck Gold and the Hawkins Glacier Dall Rams.

Cleaning up the airdrop mess.

Me, standing on Hawkins Glacier Moraine.

Tom Spurnak's Interstate.

AN ABSAROKA ELK

The same year as my last sheep hunt, I had arranged to go elk hunting in Wyoming. It was a November hunt. My guide was Randy Olson, whose father I had met in Anchorage. Randy had a guiding service and operated out of Cody, Wyoming.

My usual habit, when I traveled to hunt for ducks, geese, woodcock, or partridge, was to separate my shotgun barrel from the stock. Then I stuffed the parts into the center of my old Army duffel bag and packed my clothes around them. All my previous hunts with my trusty 7mm Remington had been in Alaska, so there was never a need to take it apart. Before I left Anchorage to fly to Cody, I went to the rifle range and rechecked my 200-yard sighting pattern. All seemed to be in order, so I took the rifle barrel and stock apart and packed them in the duffel bag.

I arrived in Cody and was met by Randy. He informed me that there were two other hunters in the party, a civil engineer from Denver and a hunter from Germany. They were hunting for a trophy elk, whereas I would be happy with any decent-sized bull.

Cody was one of the last western towns to be settled. Buffalo Bill Cody, who the town was named after, was famous as a buffalo hunter, scout, and showman. With a group of other entrepreneurs, he founded the town about 1900. The Arapaho, Crow, Cheyenne, and Shoshone Indian tribes had lived and hunted in this area long before it became Cody. It was a hunting and fishing paradise ... with plenty of land for ranchers and farmers. Irrigation was provided by the Shoshone River. The valleys and rivers created an eastern gateway to Yellowstone National Park.

Randy put us up in the famous Irma Hotel—named after Buffalo Bill's youngest daughter—built in 1902. We had lunch in the historic Cherry Bar, named after the cherry wood bar that Queen Victoria had given to Buffalo Bill. While there, in conversation about our hunt, the subject of going to a local range to sight in our rifles was brought up. We all declined the offer since this had already been done.

Early the next morning, we drove 40 miles west to Randy's corral along the South Fork of the Shoshone River. During the drive, I saw deer, elk, Bighorn Sheep, and distant antelope. Randy had said we would see lots of game and that, per square mile, Wyoming exceeded Alaska by far. I had to agree with him.

We arrived at the corral and saddled our horses. My knowledge of horses was zero, except for "Giddy up, whoa, gee, and haw" and I'm not too sure about the last two commands. I watched in amazement as Randy and B. J. Coy, my guide, tied panyards on Popcorn and two smaller mules. I learned that securing the loads on the pack animals is a rope art that the cowboys have perfected over many years. They take great pride in their skill and speed to do this.

There were six of us on horseback. Popcorn, a large mule, was tied to my saddle horn, and the other mules were led by B.J., who was last in line. Randy and his wife Ginger, led us as we headed west into the Absaroka Wilderness area. It was a beautiful fall "football" day, with temperatures in the high 40s. The mountain trail led along the South Fork of the Shoshone River. We were slowly climbing higher through meadows and pine forests and crossing several streams. There was one very narrow section of trail where a landslide had occurred. With one misstep, you and your horse were going to fall 1000 feet into the stream below. It was, all in all, a comfortable six-hour ride to our base camp—in a beautiful stand of pine trees at an altitude of about 7500 feet. The camp consisted of a large mess tent, a tack tent, a guide's tent, outfitter's tent, biffy tent, shower tent, several hunter tents, and a corral.

Wilderness areas have strict usage rules that apply to everyone, and especially to guides and hunters. No mechanical or motorized equipment was allowed. Also, camp location, party size, fires, and garbage disposal, were all strictly regulated by the U.S. Forest Service. Randy and the guides had to get special permission to go back into the camp area during the summer to cut firewood with a chainsaw for use in the hunting season. All cooking and heating were done by a wood fire. A Coleman lantern was allowed to light the cook tent.

Our guides came to our tents at 5 a.m. to wake us up and start a fire in our small wood stoves. The night time temperatures dropped into the 20s, so I was glad to have my down sleeping bag. When the tent had warmed up, we got dressed, and then headed to the mess tent for a "cowboy" breakfast prepared by Ginger. It consisted of coffee—so strong it would take the enamel off your teeth, juice, eggs any style, sausage, bacon, pancakes or waffles, many kinds of cereal, stacks of toast, and several kinds of jam. This was pretty "cushy" camp living!

After breakfast, the guides saddled up the horses and agreed as to what area each was going to hunt. We mounted up and left camp in the dark. All the guides were rodeo riders, and knew intimately the nature of our horses. They knew when your steed was giving you his best, and when he was bagging it. It was a total mystery to me. I did learn that my horse liked carrots. That's about it.

B.J. wanted us to reach a certain area before light, because the best chance for a shot was in the early morning or waning light of evening. Our first day out was a total bust. We didn't see any elk or sign of elk.

The next morning, B.J. wanted to hunt a high-altitude area. It was at least a three hour ride away. By midmorning, we reached a stand of large pine trees with converging mountain streams and waterfalls. At this altitude, 9500 feet, there was plenty of snow. I got off my horse to walk around and stretch my legs—just poking around taking in all the beauty ... when I saw a large pine tree that had a huge circular slash of bark removed. I went over to investigate it. Carved deeply into the slashed area—was the year 1895. B.J. said it was probably carved by the first survey party in this area, some 88 years earlier.

From there, we headed out onto a wide valley floor that had scattered stands of trees. I could see the peaks of the Continental Divide to our west. I'm guessing they were 12,000 feet high. B.J. was constantly scoping a high bench above us, toward where we were heading. We pulled into a small stand of pines, and B.J. had me wait there. When he returned, he said there was a whole herd of elk up on the bench—some 600 yards ahead of us. There was no cover between us and the elk. B.J. said I had to do a "Jeremiah Johnson" to keep out of the elk's view. The sight of men on horseback was enough to spook the elk. Okay, so what's a "Jeremiah Johnson"? I got a quick lesson. Between tree stands, I am to hold on to my saddle horn and lean down across my horse's side, out of sight of the elk. We rode from tree stand to tree stand in this awkward position—heading toward the elk to get under their line of vision. All went well, except when the distances between tree stands were long. Several times, I thought I was going to lose my grip and fall to the ground. We finally reached an area under the elk's line of sight. B.J. then led me up a long valley, because, he said, sometimes the bulls separate from the herd, and it was worth the effort to check this possibility out. We spent about a half hour on this venture with no luck.

We turned around to retrace our steps and started to climb the mountainside. At this tree line altitude of about 10,000 feet, cover was sparse, so we had to keep below the ridge line just ahead of us. B.J. had us tie our horses to a group of scrub pines, and said to me, "Ok, now it's 'Go and Blow time!'" I sort of knew what he meant, and wished I were in better physical shape. I also wished I was carrying a five pound .267 rifle instead of my eight pound 7mm.

We hustled up the steep slope for about 200 yards stopping for a breather when I said "Uncle." At this point, B.J. crawled to the ridge line for a peek at our prey. He pointed higher and led us up another 50 yards. By now my heart was pounding and I was breathing like I had just run a 100-yard dash. We both crawled to the ridge and peeked over.

There, about 150 yards from us, lay at least 200 elk; a hunter's dream. Some were in family groups, others just scattered about in the huge sprawling assembly—all chewing their cud and unaware of us. B.J. whispered to me to just lay still, and take a breather, so I could make a steady shot. He then began to point out to me several big bulls—which, as hard as I tried, I could not figure out. When I had calmed down a bit, I began to look through my 10-power scope in order to pick out the bulls B.J. was talking about. My inexperience as an elk hunter was working against me as I still couldn't spot the biggest bulls. B.J. was getting a bit exasperated with me ... so, he described several circles of cows, which I could make out, and in the middle was my trophy. Okay, I got the message.

I picked out the closest and largest 4X4 antlered bull. The adrenalin was dripping from my earlobes as I brought the cross hairs of my scope to the shoulder of the unsuspecting bull. My heart was pounding, and holding a steady aim was difficult. B.J. was peering through his binoculars at my target. I slowly squeezed off a shot. POW!!!

B.J., said "You missed him." All the elk stood up. I squeezed off another shot. POW!!! Another miss. All the elk turned and began to walk away from us. I took aim at my now walking bull and fired another shot—another miss! Now the herd began to trot away.

My exasperated guide said, "Gimme your rifle!" B.J. shot two more times at my bull—still no luck. By now the whole herd was trotting out of range. We stood there in silence and watched till they were out of sight.

B.J. handed me my rifle, I could see he was holding back his disgust with my missing such an easy shot. He said, "Tell me about this rifle, how you've handled it since you left Anchorage?"

Through tears I explained how I had gone to the range and sighted it in at 200 yards, then had taken it apart and put it in my duffel bag with clothes packed all around it. When I got to my room in the Irma, I just put it back together.

B.J. then explained to me that when I put the rifle back together, I had to resight it in because the barrel seating in the stock would be different and this changed the trajectory of the bullet.

Why didn't I learn this years ago? Needless to say, two very disappointed and very quiet hunters returned to camp to tell the sad story around the dinner table.

The snow began to fall in earnest during the night and accumulated to about six inches by morning. This seemed to encourage everyone as we could now see the animal tracks. I was given a .267 caliber rifle that belonged to one of the other guides. After my experience from the previous day my enthusiasm really wasn't what it should have been. I felt like I did when Ohio State beat Michigan. I could sense there was an unspoken competition and pride of achievement among the guides to see whose hunter brought in the biggest trophy. I felt I had let my guide down, especially since I had taken many previous big game animals with my trusty 7mm. Well … "RATS!" Buck up Richard.—"Go Blue Boys"—do not give up.

The next morning, B.J. led me out in the cold darkness. We followed old trails that he probably knew by heart. I just let my horse follow along. There were stretches when we went through timber, and the horses had to step over dead, fallen trees. In the darkness there was always the danger of getting knocked off my horse by a branch in the face. We spent the day mostly on our steeds, checking out valleys with no luck. Just at the last light of day, B.J. spotted a forked horn bull in the timber above us. We dismounted, tied up our horses, and quietly crept for a closer shot. At 100 yards, B. J. tried to point out the bull, but, as on the previous day, I was having a hard time looking up through the brush to see my target. Daylight was fast fading, and I had to get a shot off, or go back to camp with a frustrated guide and be skunked again. With B.J.'s pointing out various tree and branch shapes, I located the elk. I could only make out his front legs and head. I found a small branch for a rest, and with some trepidation, squeezed off a shot. B.J. shouted, "You got him in the leg!" I couldn't tell if I had even hit my target. My guide had 10-power eyes and 20-years of experience, so I believed him. The elk had fallen to the ground but was fully alert and could move about. It was too dark now and I could not get a good look for another shot. B.J. said he was sure the wounded bull was going to stay where he was for the night. We would come back in the morning and get him. My mood was much better, and I enjoyed the joshing, joking, and volumes of BS that were always a part of the dinner table in hunting camps. The other two hunters had not seen an elk that had satisfied their size for a trophy, so I was the only one with a story to tell. I should probably say … an "incomplete" story to tell.

The next morning, we headed back to my downed elk. B.J. had the mind of an elk, and positioned me where he felt the elk might travel when he drove him out of his resting place. Then off he went, and I remained alert and ready to give this boy the coup de gras. The mountains of Absaroka were stone silent as I waited for the bull to appear. About a half hour later, B.J. appeared and queried me about seeing the elk. "Nada, zero, zip, zilch" I said.

He said, "Okay, wait here. I saw your elk; he's in bad shape. I'll bring him back to you." I couldn't believe the confidence of an experienced guide. Sure enough, within an hour, B.J. came back with my elk. It was a respectable forked horn. Good for the dinner table. We did some skinning and butchering and headed back to camp.

The following morning, we were up early and prepared to return to Cody. The snow accumulation was nearly 10 inches and the temperature did not reach higher than 15 degrees that day. Everyone in camp was busy at some task in order for us to leave as early as possible. If I had known what was ahead for that day, I would have crawled back into my sleeping bag and waited for a warmer day. The guides tied panyards on each of the six mules that were to go back with us. Popcorn, my friendly mule companion, was again tied to my saddle horn. At 10:30 a.m. we were ready to pull out. Our long line had our outfitter Randy and his wife Ginger in the lead, with the six mules tied together and their lead line attached to Ginger's saddle horn. Then came we three hunters, with Popcorn and me being the last hunter, followed by B. J., who was at the end of our long line. Farewells were given to those remaining behind to close up camp, and our long trek back to the corral began.

The trail took us to the first stream we needed to cross. It was about 50 feet wide, no more than three feet deep, and was within eyesight of the camp. You will remember that our first six-hour trek in was done on a pleasant, sunny day, with temperatures in the high 40s. Stream crossings then were without any difficulty. Today, however, it was a different story. At these freezing temperatures, ice had begun to form along the stream banks and extended out into the stream three or four feet. The middle and deeper part of the stream was ice free. I watched as Randy led his horse out onto the thin ice at the stream's edge. It quickly became apparent that horses do not like to step on thin ice that they break through, not knowing how deep it was to good footing. Randy had to urge his resistant steed ahead, to make a trail of broken ice, so the rest of us could follow. All was well. Randy and Ginger reached the far side, with the first mule coming out of the water right behind Ginger. Mules 2 through 5 were out in the water spanning the stream, and mule 6 was just entering the water. Without warning, one of the mules in the middle of the stream, lost its footing, and fell sideways pulling down the mules it was tied to. The result was "Mule Chaos" in the middle of the stream. There was jerking, pulling, and baying like I have never seen or heard before. Randy and B.J. jumped into the stream to restore order. Guys from the camp came running over to help. Finally, after about 45 minutes, the mules were assembled on the far bank. What should have taken us five minutes had burned up three quarters of an hour. We never repeated the disaster that occurred at the first stream, but every stream crossing thereafter took more time than it had on the trail into camp. As we descended to lower altitudes, each stream was wider.

By midafternoon, it began to snow again, and I could feel the temperature dropping towards zero. Memories of my Army tour in Alaska some 30 years earlier began to roll around in my brain. I knew how to dress for cold weather, and I was layered with wool and goose down to withstand below zero temperatures. However, there was one serious problem I didn't count on—sitting on horseback for hours at a time became a freezing experience. My circulatory system at 50, was obviously not as good as when I was 20 and slept out in Alaska at

63 degrees below zero! Several times I attempted to walk behind my horse in order to warm up. This proved to be futile because my horse's natural gait was faster than I could walk. I needed to do a half jog, which didn't work either, so I settled for just staying cold. Randy had us stop several times and check each other for signs of frostbite.

We were not making good time, and our sunlight was gone by 5 p.m. The light snowfall continued and the wind was enough to add snow drifts along the trail. By 7 or 8 p.m., we reached the most dangerous part of the trail where a wrong step could send us and our horses 1000 feet down into the creek below. Horses, and probably mules, are smart enough to know it's easier to walk in shallow snow than plow through the deep stuff. Of course, the least snow was right at the downhill edge of our now snow covered trail. Randy and Ginger were still in the lead, and brought our frozen caravan to a halt. B.J. and Randy exchanged a few words, then Randy took a coal shovel that he had strapped to the side of his horse and began the task of shoveling out our drifted trail. I know he shoveled for at least 50 yards before B.J. took over. This was a Herculean task of great strength and stamina. I couldn't believe what I was seeing and that they would even think to do this. It obviously saved our bacon, as now the horses were willing to stay on the safe ground instead of preferring to walk along the trail's downhill edge.

We slowly descended out of the Absaroka Mountains to the flat riverbed of the Shoshone River—a ghost-like column … slowly moving along with muffled sounds of hoofs on snow … and leather saddles rubbing against man and beast. It was now about midnight. We had been traveling for 13 hours and still hadn't reached the corral. I was frozen and concerned about frostbite. The temperature must have been near zero or below. It had stopped snowing and there was no wind. A full moon had added its light to the ambient light of the snow-covered ground. I had no idea how much further we had to go but was in serious prayer that it wasn't much. We plodded along … following our leader on the bank of the Shoshone which now was wide with braids of streams. Randy attempted to cross the river several times, but it was too deep. We continued downstream looking for a shallower crossing.

A light on a high pole appeared in the distance. We were now in ranch country as an occasional fence appeared. I remembered that we did cut one fence in order to head for the light. This is a "No-No" in cow country. Randy had us wait while he and B.J. took off on foot to see if we should head for the light or cross the river. They soon returned and described the irrigation ditches between us and the light. The ditches were about 12 inches wide and two or three feet deep. They were a "broken leg" hazard for a horse.

Randy finally found a place to cross the river. It was wide and glistened like diamonds in the moonlight. It was shallow enough to not spook the mules, which was critical. Then, a short time later, the welcoming sight of the corral appeared. Hallelujah! Now began the work of unsaddling, unpacking, loading up the vehicles, and getting all the beasts of burden fed and bedded down. They had surely earned their keep this night.

We were a noisy and happy bunch as we cranked up the engines for an hour drive back to Cody. The Irma Hotel was a most welcome sight at 3 a.m. I am averse to hot showers and baths, but, let me tell you, "Bucky," I slid my frozen body into a tub of boiling hot water that night. I came out like a cooked lobster and very glad to be alive.

Thirty-eight years later I'm looking up at my fork horn elk mount and reliving this story. It's no trophy to crow about, but the story is well worth the effort and guide fee. Besides … I know … that the 4X4 bull Elk I missed, is very happy to be living on for many more years, helping to increase the herd.

THE SINGING SAMARITAN

One of the gifts God has blessed me with is my tenor voice. I regret not having used it to serve Him instead of just enjoying singing. My primary problem was a strong fear of speaking or singing before a public audience. I mentioned this in a previous chapter.

After Sali and I were married the first time, we attended an Episcopal Church in Ypsilanti and sang in the choir. Then in Anchorage, we sang in Saint Mary's choir, and in Delafield, Wisconsin, where we live now, we sang in our Mercy Hill Church choir last Christmas.

When we were first in Alaska in the little town of Petersburg, on Mitkof Island, the high school band director recruited us and 16 others, to sing in a performance of the *Messiah*. In one of the 43 years I flew up to Nome, I sang in the *Messiah* put on by a local church. This was a rare happening for Nome, Alaska.

My musical career began in the fifth grade when the band director, Mr. Flowers, talked me into playing a clarinet. I made an attempt to read music but never became very proficient at it. To this day, I still sing by ear. If I hear a song sung I can usually pick up the notes. In something like the *Messiah* I need to position myself next to a good tenor or between two tenors, and follow along.

During the 10 years Sali and I were divorced, I sang in St Mary's choir. Our choir director was involved in the Anchorage community performing arts and approached me with a request to audition for the Anchorage Community Chorus. The chorus was going to sing with the Anchorage Symphony Orchestra in a performance of Haydn's, *The Seasons*. As you might expect, I immediately choked. I assumed they must be really hurting for tenors to reach out for someone like me. At our choir director's insistence, I agreed to audition.

I was given a phone number to call for an audition appointment. The Anchorage Performing Arts organization had, what I'd call, a small warehouse down amongst the railroad tracks in Anchorage's industrial center. All the auditions were given there. With much trepidation, I made my appointment and tried to forget my stage-fright issues.

Two weeks later, I was walking up and down the railroad tracks alongside the Symphony's warehouse. I could hear the trained voices of those auditioning offering up their chosen vocal piece. As I listened, my primary thought was, *What was I doing here? This is way out of my league. Compared to what I am hearing I'm just a "croaker." I need to get back in my car and drive off.* But then the thought came … *Michigan guys do not give up!*

My turn came soon enough. I entered the warehouse to be greeted by a young woman who had me on her list of appointments. She took me into the audition area and introduced me to Alvera Voth who was the director of the Community Chorus and would audition me.

I had never met Alvera Voth and, had I known of her resumé, I might never have shown up. She deserves her own chapter and probably a book. My research revealed that she grew up in a small Kansas farming community. She had a Master's degree in Music Education from Northwestern University. She was a pioneer in musical artistry in Alaska. She founded musical organizations throughout Alaska. She led Alaskan choral groups to sing in Washington D.C. and even Russia. She was considered a brilliant and inspiring teacher who had a great sense of humor and was an engaging public speaker. She taught at Alaska Methodist University and at the University of Alaska. After her retirement in 1995, she returned to Kansas and founded "Arts in Prison," which brought choral music to prisoners throughout Kansas. This effort, which still exists, was very successful in rehabilitating inmates. It changed many lives forever.

Fortunately, I had no knowledge of these facts as Alvera led me to the piano and bid me to sit next to her. Then came the question, "Have you brought your music? What do you plan to sing, Richard?"

The frog croaked out, "Ah … Ah … well … well, I don't read music and was going to let you suggest something."

Alvera quietly turned to the keyboard and began to play scales and I joined in. After a few "do-re-mi's," she asked me if there was a song I could sing. I said, "I can sing Danny Boy." She began to play the song and I entered in. About halfway through she stopped and turned to me.

"Well, Richard … I've been auditioning all these people with trained voices. They have the formal training, voice lessons, and experience. You have no training, no voice lessons, only some church choir experience, but … you do have the voice. Welcome to our tenor section."

The performance of Haydn's "The Seasons" was given in the Wendy Williamson Auditorium on the University of Alaska–Anchorage campus. It was a very, very cold January night. The temperatures were down in the 10 to 20 degrees below zero range.

I got a haircut, dug out my seldom-worn tuxedo, and dressed as required for the chorus members. We assembled on stage along with the symphony orchestra and performed to a full house. As I remember back about 40 years ago, I think we got a standing ovation at the end of the performance.

The Anchorage Performing Arts organization had a well-attended "Tea" following the performance. I rubbed elbows with the attending dignitaries as I had my "Tea and Crumpets" and absorbed a few compliments.

The time now was slightly past midnight. I bundled up with my overcoat, scarf, gloves, and headed for my car. Foolishly, I wore no hat. I couldn't mess up my hair for the performance. The patent leather shoes offered no warmth, and at 20 degrees below zero, it felt like I was barefoot.

My beloved BMW started right up, and I headed for home about seven miles away. There was no traffic at that time of night. The way home was lit by stop lights and street lights. I was approaching a well-lit neighborhood intersection, when I saw a man lying in the street. Immediately my thoughts were, this guy's going to freeze to death unless I get him in the car.

I pulled over, hopped out of the car, and headed for the downed guy. I reached down, shook his shoulder and yelled for him to get up. No response ... it was like he was unconscious. With some effort I pulled him up to a sitting position and kept talking to him in a loud voice. He began to mumble something. He was obviously very drunk. A little more lifting and tugging and I got him to his feet. Then, with no help from my patent leather shoes, I maneuvered him to my car. It took all my strength to hold him up, open the car door, and get him into the passenger seat.

We just sat there for a while as he warmed up. I finally was able to get him to understand that I needed to know where he lived. He mumbled out some directions, so I headed down the street, hoping to find his home. This went on for about a half an hour with no success. During this time he began to sober up a bit.

Also during this time my BMW heater began to blow out cold air. I checked the dash heater gauge and it was indicating that the engine temperature was slightly above normal. I turned the fan speed down and the heater gauge higher with some success of warmer air. My hope was that at twenty below the cold air would keep the engine temperature down.

It took another half hour to finally find my passenger's home. By then, only cold air was coming out of the heater and the engine temperature needle was as high as it could measure, up to boiling point! It was now 1:30 a.m., and I was four miles from home. I wasn't dressed for a long hike home, and I had no phone to call a taxi. My only choice was to drive home with an overheated engine.

The next morning I called Ginny, one of my orthodontic assistants who lived nearby, and told her I needed her to come over and follow me to a garage that had previously repaired my BMW. I had left the car parked outside, so I started it with a very cold engine. I hoped that in the five miles we had to go the engine would not overheat. No such luck. As I drove along, I watched the engine temperature climb to the maximum reading.

I received a call at work about noon from the garage owner. He gave me the bad news. He found a tiny leak in the radiator which, over a long period of time, caused the loss of the antifreeze. The engine was a total loss. The estimate to replace it was $6,000. I liked my BMW, but it wasn't a classic and not a potential collector's item, so I put it up "FOR SALE as is."

So there you have my Singing Samaritan story. A man's life was saved and a BMW was lost.

MURPHY

Towards the end of my bachelor life I decided to go to a dog show in downtown Anchorage. We had owned two English Setters, four

Labrador Retrievers, and our beloved Fluffy, a blonde, mixed-Terrier breed dog, whose wistful brown eyes drew us to her at the dog pound. She lived with us for 17 years. It was a very tearful day for our family when I had to take her to the vet and say goodbye.

I sat up in the bleachers of the dog show and watched the obedience performance and lengthy, best-of-breed judging. I was drawn to the Scottish Terriers that were being shown. All the dog owners had an assigned area in which to groom and keep their dogs ... so I decided to visit a few Scottie owners to see if they had any Scotties for sale.

This led me to Sally Johnson, a breeder, who said she had a litter of Scottie pups that soon could be purchased. After interviewing me to satisfy her that I was a qualified buyer, she invited me to come and see the litter. I checked out the four pups that were left, from a litter of six, and really couldn't decide which one to purchase. Sally's selection for me was a little, rather reserved male. She said people who are going to show their Scotties want a more aggressive, "I own this place" dog, whereas I wanted an enjoyable companion. I agreed with her advice and purchased the male she selected. The name "MURPHY" was written all over him, so no other choice was considered. It proved to be the perfect name.

I had no experience with Scottish Terriers. I did not know that they were: 1. Hard to potty train, 2. Notably independent, 3. Not friendly with other dogs, 4. Not very affectionate, 5. Known to bark a lot, and 6. Seldom seen in an obedience group at a dog show.

In reading about Scotties, I discovered that they are not good swimmers due to their large head and short legs. I also discovered that Murphy couldn't keep up with me in wet snow when I took him cross-country skiing on ungroomed trails. The wet snow packed under his belly and around his short little legs bringing him to a halt. I had to pick him up and carry him home. Then I put him in a tub of warm water to melt off all the snow.

Contrary to reputation, Murphy was easily potty trained. It took only two weeks to train him that we go to the potty outdoors. His good traits were that he loved children, and he loved to catch a thrown frisbee.

He always had a happy disposition and basically got along with other dogs. He was friendly to everyone but did not seek affection. However, he didn't resist being petted or held. Yes, he did have a mind of his own. When I called him, "Hey Murph, come over here." His reaction was to look at me, then continue whatever he was doing. Then … in due time … he'd trot over, "Yes, you called me?" Another habit he had was at bedtime. I'd have him go into his little travel pen next to my bed. "Good night, Murph." I'd be asleep in five minutes and thought Murphy was too. Not so… I discovered that after I was asleep he went downstairs and spent the night on the back of my living room couch. There he watched out of the large living room window for anything that might come by. On several nights his barking would wake me. I'd run down the stairs and see a large moose had wandered into view.

On my working days, I'd take Murphy to my orthodontic office. It wasn't professional to have a dog running around the operatory, so I trained Murphy to stay in my personal office or in the staff room. He caught on and rarely disobeyed.

It didn't take long before the kids and my adult patients found out that there was a Scottie dog in the office. They often asked if they could go see Murphy. As long as the parents approved and they stayed in the staff room, we allowed this.

I remember one family, who were all in braces, always wanted to see Murphy. The father was a very large, manly guy who came in on different days. He'd always ask in his deep bass voice, "Is Murphy here?" When the answer was, "Yes," he always went back to visit Murphy.

At the end of the day, we'd occasionally let the last few patients bring Murphy out into the operatory where they could run and chase one another. It was all in fun, and we never had any complaints. I began to think that Murphy's orthodontic practice was becoming as large as mine.

Murphy's first boat ride was on Alexander Creek, across the inlet from Anchorage. "Well Murph, you might as well come along with Sali and me." I had rented a 16-foot river punt with a 30-horse outboard, we loaded up our gear, and hopped in to try our luck fishing. I put Murphy in the boat and he climbed up on the bow seat. Off we went. I got our speed up to a plane and headed to our fishing destination. With no warning … suddenly Murphy fell into the water. I knew he couldn't swim well, and that I couldn't quickly turn the boat around. I looked down into the murky water just over the side and saw, quickly passing by a black ball of hair. I made a grab for it … and miraculously got a hold of enough hair to pull Murph up and aboard the boat. You can imagine how thankful and happy Sali and I were at that moment. No more bow seats for Murph.

There were times when I would take Murphy out to my Iliamna Lake cabin near Pedro Bay. He was a good flyer and enjoyed these trips. On one occasion, I brought along two of my grandsons … Justin, 10, and Jordan, 8. I was up early one morning making coffee, and the boys were still asleep in the loft. Murphy began to growl, and I wondered why. Foolishly, instead of looking out the window, I opened the door to let him out on the deck. He flew out the door … barking and barking. I looked out of the window and there was Murphy on the edge of the deck and a big Brown bear turning to run off. I forgot to mention earlier that terriers are known to be fearless, and this was a perfect example. It's an admirable trait, but I did not want to lose my buddy by making a foolish mistake like this one … pitting my 20-pound Murphy against an 800-pound Brown bear.

A year or two later, the boys and I were at the cabin again. One day we were out in my boat scouting around for sockeye salmon to catch. I had made us a lunch so we decided to have our picnic on a beautiful stony beach. Murphy was running around sniffing out the place as we ate our sandwiches. I was gazing around this large cove and spotted a Brown bear moving up to a large rock outcropping. I told the boys to quick get in the boat and get their camera ready. They put Murphy in the boat and we shoved off. By then the bear was in the water swimming across the bay. I motored us to the swimming bear and slowly circled him as he paddled toward the other shore. Murphy was focused on the bear and growling. My grandsons were enjoying this unusual experience.

Mr. Brown bear swam to the shore and climbed up a steep moss and lichen covered bank. With his rear end towards us and turning his head to look at us, he lifted one hind leg and relieved himself, as if to say, "You guys didn't scare me. I saw your rifle. I saw your dog, but I know I could have eaten your dog, eaten what's left of your lunch, and you too, if you didn't somehow get away. This is my territory. I've been here all my life. Now, I don't mind if you take a few fish, but leave me enough to survive the coming winter."

Lastly … there's this little romantic story I must share with you. Murphy was always this perfect little gentleman around female dogs even though he was not neutered. He easily qualified for admittance to a monastery. While we were living on Hideaway Lake Drive, on an acre and a quarter lot up the mountainside, I occasionally let Murphy wander around outside with minimal supervision. One day I called for him … then I looked for him … alas, no Murphy. That evening he still hadn't returned and we began to worry. There were bears in the area and the neighbors Labrador had once chewed Fluffy up to a point of near death.

The next morning I drove around the neighborhood hoping to find my buddy. My last look was on the street above us. There he was, out in the front yard of a house directly above us. Not alone, but sitting next to him was a grey Schnauzer about his size. The lady of the house came out to greet me as I was walking to pick up Murphy. She said Murphy had spent the night with Molly and they were happy for the occasion. As I drove home, I asked Murph what was going on; why couldn't he find his way back home? He seemed unconcerned.

Over the years that we lived in the Hideaway house, Murphy often made his way up to visit his girlfriend, Molly. Only once did he come home by himself. One evening that Murphy had disappeared, I drove up to find him. There in Molly's front yard sat Molly and Murphy at the gravel road's edge. Behind them, about 30 feet away, were at least seven wild rabbits eating the lawn grass. A couple of fine hunting dogs, don't you think? Molly's owner appeared and informed me that Molly was teaching Murphy how to chase cars. I just laughed and took my wayward child home again.

The final instance I can remember, was a time when Murphy didn't come home and I decided to just let him be gone. A week later I drove up to Molly's, but no dogs were in the yard. I knocked on the door and was welcomed in. Molly and Murphy looked up at me as if to say, "We're doing just fine, don't worry about us." Molly's owner said, "You know, we love Murphy, and we would be glad to keep him." I said that I appreciated their caring for him, but I could never give him up.

We sold our Hideaway house and moved to Girdwood in January of 2000. Murphy was now about 10 years old. He had been diagnosed with Cushing's disease a year before we moved. This disease is usually found in older dogs and is caused by a tumor, malignant or nonmalignant, on the pituitary gland. It occurs in both humans and animals. A dog's life span after diagnosis is four years. Oddly, he didn't show any significant signs of having the disease. He was just his happy little Scottie dog self.

Girdwood is a mountain ski resort 34 miles from Anchorage. It has a wet climate which turns to lots of snow in the winter. It is graced with tall stands of Spruce and Hemlock trees. The dense trees behind our house were Murphy's favorite place to explore.

One beautiful fall afternoon I went out behind our house to call Murphy. He didn't respond, so I walked over to the neighbors behind our house to see if Murph was there visiting their dogs. The neighbor said he hadn't seen Murph, so I asked him if I could explore the woods behind his house They were contiguous with our woods and I could walk through them back to our house. The ground under the tree canopy was covered with moss, ferns, Devils Club, blueberries, and had small pockets of water under fallen upturned tree roots. Very little sunshine penetrated this tree canopy. It was a very Hobbit-like, Rain Forest place. This was a perfect place for a Scottish Terrier. They were bred by farmers to go after vermin, badgers and fox. They, fearlessly, went right down into their dens to root them out.

I took my time just poking around the forest area, looking here and there and softly calling out Murphy's name. I probably spent a half hour slowly making my way towards our house. I wasn't far from home when I discovered Murph, Murphel-do, my little Woodie guy. He had curled up at the base of a tree for his last long nap. Oh Murph, you were such a good guy. Such a happy Scottie.

With streams of tears running down my face, I picked him up and carried him to the back of our house. Sali had come out on the second story back porch. I held Murphy up to her, and we cried. Sleep well Murph, sleep well my dear little friend. God will take care of you.

Our grandkids loved Murphy.

Brittney.

Jordan.

MURPHY

Hey Murph, Mister Woodro
Such a guy, such a good guy you were
Such little legs
Dark innocent eyes hidden behind those long eyebrows
Ears and tail that stuck straight up
And what a long nose you had
What a neat beard

Such a gentlemen you were too
When I talked serious with you
You cocked your head right to left, left to right
Like you were trying hard to understand what I was saying

Kids ... You always loved kids
How fun it was to watch you grab a mitten or sock
And run back and forth, round and round
Remember how you ran to catch a Frisbee I would throw
That was great fun!

Such a Woodie guy you were
How you loved to ride in my truck
Hanging out the window to get a smell
Attracting great attentions and laughs at stop lights
Then there was your girlfriend, Molly
The little Schnauzer who lived up the hill
You, "Little Rat," always running off to Molly's
At least I knew where to find you
Never understood why it was always a one-way trip
You never could find your way back home

Hey Murph, Murphel-do
Happy little Scottie
Such a tail-wager
Even on this last day of your life
You were happy

Then in typical Scottie fashion
Independent to the end
You wandered off into the woods behind the house
To take your last long nap
Sleep well, my little buddy
Such a guy, such a good, good guy

LIFETIME FRIEND

To have known Jack Rudell is an adventure in itself. We met at "The University of Michigan Dental School." Jack had served in the U.S. Air Force in France at about the same time I was in the Army in Alaska. According to Jack, he rescued the love of his life, Anne Marie, "Mrs. Woodie," or "My Little French Somesing," when he found her buried head-first in a snowbank while skiing in the Alps. They married and went on to have three sons; Jean Pierre—"Mr. Pierre," Jean Paul—"Squeeky Buggers," and Jacques Christophe—"Manzie Mouse." As you can tell, Jack could not resist giving his closest loved one's nicknames. This, of course, was born out of deep love and affection. As his sons grew to manhood, he had to abandon these cherished childhood names. I ask their forgiveness for making them public. They are now our "adopted" sons. Sali and I have a great love for them and Anne.

Jack and I met in our dental school dental lab when we were assigned opposite lab desks. We were very close in age and had much in common … he being from Wisconsin, and me, from Michigan. I cannot remember the origin, but Jack's humor and mine clicked when we began to do extemporaneous skits related to a popular radio program entitled "Amos and Andy." This situational comedy show was a nightly occurrence until the early 1950s. It was, by today's standards, totally "politically incorrect" and wouldn't be allowed on the air.

In our skits, one of us was "Amos," and the other "Andy," and we always included the girlfriend, "Sapphire." We were working away on our dental lab assignment, conversing along the way, and Jack was often smoking a cigarette, (allowed in the 1950s), when suddenly … Amos or Andy appeared as if they had just walked into the lab. We were never exactly certain where we were going with our production and plot. "The Sapphire" was always central to our skits. Some scoundrel was always enticing her to run off and leave her husband, "The Kingfish." There were brother-in-law problems, financial problems, (usually related to excessive shopping), seeing the doctor problems, and any human life tribulation we could dream up and try to work our way out of. By the time we had worked out the problem, our gathered classmates were laughing to the point of tears.

After dental school graduation, Jack chose to practice dentistry in Grand Rapids, Michigan, Sali's hometown. From an earlier chapter you learned that I chose to practice in Petersburg—a small, Norwegian fishing village on Mitkof Island in Southeast Alaska. Our friendship went on; family dinners of excellent French cuisine prepared by Annie, when we visited Sali's mother in Grand Rapids ... hunting and fishing excursions ... trips to Chicago ... visits to Alaska ... and eventually, a business partnership and corporation. Often I was working, and the phone rang, "This is Rudell, you got a minute?" Jack then proceeded to tell me about some piece of property in Grand Rapids that we should buy. One small house that we bought together had been owned by the Salvation Army. Somewhere inside, Jack found a wide, black leather belt with an ornate real silver buckle engraved with the Salvation Army emblem on it. The belt became a sort of Presidential Gavel that was traded back and forth as we alternately became president of our corporation. It was such fun!

From buying land, we went on to build a couple professional buildings. One building, on Alpine Avenue in Grand Rapids, was erroneously staked out and built 13 feet too close to the road. Our unhappy neighbor, a MacDonald's owner, complained to the Walker City Board that our building was blocking the view to his business. The end result was that 13 feet of the front of our brick building had to be cut off. Painful.

In September 1966, Jack and Anne drove from Grand Rapids to Prince Rupert, B.C. where they boarded the ferry to Petersburg—a total distance of 2900 miles, to visit us. And ... all that way, in their small Volkswagen Bug.

Entertaining guests in Petersburg most often involved boating and fishing. So, a couple days after their arrival, we all piled into the boat I had built, and motored 25 miles down the Inside Passage to Duncan Canal. We used the U.S. Forest Service cabin located there. It was on the shore of a remote lake, surrounded by low mountains. This was rainforest country with dense stands of Hemlock and Spruce trees covering the terrain as far as we could see. Our plan was to fish the tidal outflow for cutthroat trout and silver salmon. The incoming tide filled the lake with brackish water. Then, when the tide began to flow out, it created a rapids where the cutthroat gathered to feed. We had great success using our spinning rods and orange beaded spinner baits. Nothing like a meal of fresh-caught trout.

It was late September, and mountain goat season was open, so Jack and I made plans to go goat hunting. Sali and Anne prepared our menu for the couple days we would be gone. We headed out across Frederick Sound in my boat toward Horn Cliffs—where I had hunted before. We cruised along the base of the cliffs into Le Conte Glacier Bay and navigated the boat up into the mouth of a small creek where we could anchor for the night. This same creek where I took Ron Hall, the Lemon Drop Kid, for a sleepless night. We had our excellent, but "cold," dinner, and spread our sleeping bags on the floor of the boat's small cabin. Typical of Southeast Alaska, rain drizzled down all night. I regretted not doing a better caulking job around the windows, as water dripped down onto our sleeping bags.

Le Conte Glacier is the southernmost active tidewater glacier in the world. It continually calves off huge chunks of ice that break up into smaller chunks as they float out into Frederick Sound. There have been times when wind and tidal currents have taken large ice bergs all the way some 10 or 15 miles up the sound and into Petersburg Harbor, damaging float plane hangars.

When Jack and I went to sleep, the tide was coming in, and we had three or four feet of water under us. By midnight, however, the incoming tide had lifted our boat and brought in a whole flotilla of ice chunks—the largest ones about basketball size. We were awakened by their continual banging into the side of the boat. This went on all night until the changing tide took our "ice cubes" out into the Sound. I can still hear Jack's comment: "Richard, I never thought I'd sleep all night in a Martini glass!" That was a typical "Rudell" comment. He never missed an opportunity to humorously describe a situation.

The next day, we climbed up Horn Cliffs to about 1000 feet. The weather remained high overcast and wet. There was plenty of goat sign: worn trails, hair, droppings, and the strong smell of goat. Our spirits and enthusiasm were high, as we traversed the plateau we were on. We carefully glassed the surrounding terrain for several hours, hoping to spot a large Billy, but alas—no trophies to bring home. Skunked. After a wonderful visit, we bought their VW Bug and they flew home.

Jack and I had many other fishing and hunting trips: for woodcock, partridge, pheasants, ducks, and geese. These great times took us to Iowa, northern Michigan, South Dakota, Manitoba and Saskatchewan, Canada, and Kodiak Island, Alaska. The last memorable hunt that Jack, his son Chris, and I went on, was in South Dakota. This was supposed to be a "pot hole" duck hunting trip on the Pine Ridge Reservation near Rapid City. Don't ask me how, or why, Jack meets various types of unusual "characters," but here we go again.

Jack, Chris, and I arrived at the Rapid City airport and were met by our host, Chief Buddy Red Bow. The Chief was a jovial, energetic, Lakota Indian. Rudell was always full of surprises, and Warfield Richards, "Buddy Red Bow," was another one for my quiver. I can't remember Jack's story of how he met the Chief, but obviously their conversation led to an invitation to hunt on the Pine Ridge Reservation. I always thought Indian Chiefs were tall, aged, weathered, and wise; but Buddy Red Bow was only in his late 20s and didn't fit the profile. We can't always rely on Hollywood movies to project the truth.

We rented a car and followed Buddy Red Bow all the way to the reservation where we would camp out for the next three nights. The Chief had set up a large tent with a fire pit and picnic tables for us to use. As we were turning in for the night, I stepped out in front of our tent and noticed Buddy and his girlfriend entering a small nearby house. I couldn't resist yelling to them, "Hey, Buddy, haven't we got this backwards? I thought the "white man" sleeps in the house and the Indian sleeps in the tent?" They just waved and laughed, saying, "Not here on the reservation."

The next morning, we were to do our "pot hole" shooting. I don't think that the Lakota Indians were ever seriously interested in any kind of duck hunting—probably only deer, elk, and antelope. Buddy drove us around to check out several "pot holes" It was a hot, sunny day

218

… not a "duck weather" day. We saw nothing and shot nothing. After lunch, Buddy decided to take me out for a ride around the reservation. I should mention that there were no hunting regulations on an Indian reservation—at least not on the Pine River Reservation. Buddy and I climbed into his old International and took off to hunt whatever showed up. We hadn't gone far before Buddy spotted a coyote trotting along about 100 yards from the road. He immediately headed out cross country over the grasslands at about 60 miles an hour to overtake the coyote. I can still hear him shouting, "Get ready, get ready, I'll pull alongside of him so you can get a shot." While we were bouncing along at 60, I was leaning out the passenger window with my 16-gauge pump trying to hold a bead on the flying coyote. Buddy yelled, "Take a shot, take a shot." It took me three shots at 30 yards to bring "Ole Wiley Coyote" down. We spun around to retrieve our kill. I picked up a skinny, stinky, and mangy trophy—probably my worst ever. Chief Buddy Red Bow, laughing, said, "More rabbits next year."

Sali and I have so many fond memories of times spent with the Rudells. It's a blessing to find such close friends to add color and joy to our lives. I remember our last call from Jack. He was not doing well due to a blood disease that he had fought for several years. When Sali handed me the phone, I knew that the end was near. Jack, in a raspy voice, said, "Richard, it was all good, it was all good." Then, as now, I tearfully agreed, "Yes, Jack, it was all good, it was all good." Jack died later that night.

Jack, Anne, Holly, Sali, and shy Heather.

We flew from Anchorage for Jack's farewell service held in a church in Wausau, Wisconsin, where he was born. Then we all drove to Saint Ignace, Michigan, where Anne rented a local boat along with its captain. Jack's sons, Pierre, Jean Paul, and Chris, were with us. Jack had requested that we spread his ashes in Lake Michigan under the Mackinaw Bridge. The boat captain motored us slowly out to the bridge where we spread Jack's ashes as he requested. ... "Goodbye Jack, you were such a good friend ... closer than a brother. I will miss you ... Love you man! ... Love you ..."

Proverbs 18:24b: "There is a friend who sticks closer than a brother."

That was Jack, always there for me.

Jack Rudell: His Heaven on Earth!
Photo credit: Anne Rudell.

Jack fishing on the Karluk River, Kodiak Island.

Jack Rudell and his favorite English Setter, Cedrick.

Jack and me pheasant hunting in southwest Iowa.

PART VI

AND FOUND

FORGIVENESS AND RESTORATION

The previous story "Covenant Broken" ended with my starting on a post-divorce journey in search of life, liberty, and happiness. Jack Rudell was very upset about our divorce, as were many other friends and family.

Sali launched her own "Sali's Color and Design" business. She brought beauty to many of Anchorage's homes and offices, including my office and condominium. I kept on with my orthodontic practice, straightening teeth in Anchorage and in remote Alaskan villages. The Cadillacs and Mercedes that Anchorage divorce attorneys and marriage counselors used to drive, were now worn out, and replaced by VWs and a few PT Cruisers.

Searching for happiness is a search for a fleeting thing. Perhaps this is why the framers of the Declaration of Independence phrased it as: "The pursuit of happiness." It's possible to pursue something your whole life and never achieve the result you desired. Happiness can be an event-centered, or euphoric emotion, that comes and goes like the ocean tides. Your favorite team wins its championship and you're happy. The next year they lose the championship and you're bummed. The thing that mankind really is searching for is a joy that stays with you no matter what the circumstances of life. A couple Scriptures come to mind: "The joy of the Lord is your strength!" (Nehemiah 8:10) and "Now may the God of hope fill you all with joy and peace ..." (Romans 15:13). We see in Scripture that there is a connection between hope and joy. One of Sali's personality characteristics that I liked was her joyfulness. She had a certain optimism and happiness that was contagious. I was more reserved ... not unhappy, but not as outwardly happy as she. True Believers have a deep-seated joy of the Lord. We trust God, even in times of tribulation. "Weeping may endure for a night, but joy comes in the morning" (Psalm 30:5). Jesus said, "In the world you will have tribulation" (John 16:33). I'm not sure if divorce is included in that category of tribulations, because it's a tribulation self-imposed.

During the 10 years of our divorce, we did not date each other or spend much time together except for family gatherings at Thanksgiving or Christmas, and other special family occasions … plus sporadic trips to marriage counselors. Being Christians, in the back of our minds was the desire to please God by forgiving each other and being reconciled for His Glory. My memory doesn't serve me well as to the details of our decision to get married for a second time, but there was some humor in the process. Ten years is a long time to review one's life, choices, and experiences—what works, and what doesn't. Making a commitment again to "Love and Cherish" is very hard.

My occasion to propose to Sali came under the direction of our daughter, Heather, who was aware of our serious discussions about this possibility. I had occasion to visit Sali and Heather during Heather's college spring break. She asked me if I had any serious plans with anyone concerning a relationship. I answered, "No."

Then she said, in a commanding voice, "Dad! Propose to Mom!"

I came up with a few appropriate words.

Then Heather said, "Mom! Say 'yes!'"

And Sali said, "Yes, I will."

We were all surprised and laughed—right out of the movies. Wedding plans were made; the pastors, the place, the reception dinner, and the invitation designed by Sali and taken to the printer.

Then … I got cold feet and canceled the wedding. Sali went ahead meeting with the video photographers, ordering the wedding cake, and discussing the reception menu with her friend, Suzie Stranik, our caterer. This she did in bold faith … believing the wedding would go on as planned. I was having a hard time doing what I knew was right. I knew I was disappointing Sali, my family, and friends once more. I hated to be a quitter, and our fractured family did not sit well with me. God's statement: "I hate divorce" still followed me wherever I went.

I spent the night soul-searching and seeking God for direction. I called Sali early in the morning and told her, "Go ahead and have the invitations printed, since I've already paid for them." This was an answer to her prayer. I didn't know she had stayed up all night redoing the invitation. At 6 a.m., before going to sleep, she told the Lord: "If You want me to take this invitation to the printer, You will have to have Dick call me, and tell me to take it." My call to Sali came an hour later. After one hour of sleep, Sali got up and took the invitation to the printer.

There was one BIG problem; however, it didn't change the fact that the wedding was still off. Later that day, Sali called Pastor Abe who was one of the two pastors we had asked to marry us. (Sali thought that a "Double Knot" wedding was necessary in our case.) She told him the wedding was off, and asked if he would be willing to come over and talk with us. He agreed, so Sali called me requesting I come over and meet with Abe and her. Again, I waffled around, but finally agreed to meet with Abe and Sali. Abe, being a pastor, read scriptures that pertained to the marriage covenant. I could hear this voice saying, "Do the right thing Richard." The wedding was on again—this time firmly, for good.

Sali gave me the task of stamping and mailing the invitations, thinking it would help make it a joint commitment. On May 30, 1992, we were remarried at the home of our dear friends, Suzie and Jerry Stranik. The two pastors who we asked to marry us were Rick Benjamin and Abe Jeter. Rick was Sali's Pastor at Abbott Loop Church, and Pastor Abe was a close friend of Sali's. He worked part-time at Curtis and Campbell, a paint, wallpaper, and flooring store, where Sali bought most of her supplies for her "Sali's Color and Design."

The wedding went off without a hitch. Sali was beautiful in her delicate pink midi wedding gown and pale pink headdress. I, her knight in shining armor, was in a white tux with a pink bow tie, and Murphy, my beloved black Scottie dog, behaving well, was wearing his pink bow tie. Heather was Sali's lovely matron of honor, wearing a gown of a deeper pink. Our other daughter Holly, who lived in Wisconsin, sadly was unable to attend.

Suzie Stranik provided a superb reception dinner for our gathered family and friends. The next day we flew off to Maui for our second

Honeymoon. That was 32 years ago, and yes, we made the right decision.

An epilogue to our second marriage: Two years after our remarriage, in 1994, I wanted us to have our Hepatitis C treated. Sali was unaware of the fact that she had contracted Hep C in the hospital via four blood transfusions for a bleeding ulcer about two years after our divorce. I was Cytomegalovirus negative, which made me a sought-after blood donor for the Neonatal ICU. Four or five years after our divorce, the blood bank informed me that they no longer could take my blood. They told me that I was Hepatitis C positive. I must have contracted it from a patient.

The fact that we were both Hepatitis C positive became known to us from our premarital blood tests. The treatment for this disease, at the time, was medication with Interferon and Rebetol. The doctor said we would need to have sophisticated blood tests at a cost of $600 each before the treatment could begin.

A week after the tests were taken, my doctor called, and Sali answered the phone. She heard a very excited physician exclaim, "Neither of you have Hepatitis C! You have BOTH tested NEGATIVE!" he expressed in amazement.

Sali pondered the matter, and concluded that it was surely The Lord who had healed us. It was His Wedding gift to us for our obedience to Him—by our forgiveness and reconciliation: "The mending of our broken marriage covenant with God." Another proof of His goodness toward us. For this, we offer Him praise and thanksgiving. "Now to Him who is able to do exceedingly abundantly above all that we ask or think, according to the 'Power' that works in us—to Him be glory in the church by Christ Jesus to all generations, forever and ever, Amen" (Ephesians 3: 20-21). Hallelujah!

"Sali" and Dick.
Our second marriage

"Remember ye not the former things,
neither consider the things of old.

Behold, I will do a new thing;
now it shall spring forth;
shall ye not know it?
I will even make a way in the wilderness,
and rivers in the desert."

Isaiah 43:18,19

MURPHY'S BAY CABIN

A Prayer for Murphy's Bay

Days pass and the years vanish and we walk sightless among miracles
Lord, fill our eyes with seeing and our minds with knowing.
Let there be moments when your Presence, like lightning,
illuminates the darkness in which we walk.
Help us to see, whenever we gaze,
that the bush burns, unconsumed.
And we clay touched by God,
will reach out for holiness and exclaim in wonder;
how filled with awe is this place and we did not know it.

My ideal location for a cabin in Alaska was for it to be both remote and beautiful—on a river or a lake. Even in Alaska, any cabin site accessible by road had too many hunters or fishermen to suit me. I had witnessed what we term "combat" fishing, on the Kenai River—people standing elbow to elbow, trying to snag sockeye salmon. There was always a lot of yelling, grumbling, and tangles with neighbor's lines … some fish caught and some fish lost. This was not for me.

Two years after my remarriage to Sali, the opportunity to purchase my dream cabin site beckoned me. A well-known bear guide, I'll call him Slim, brought his two children to me for orthodontic treatment. At one particular appointment, he asked me if I had ever fished out at Lake Iliamna (Illy-om-na). I told him that a fishing guide, Jim Repine, had taken me to fish the Iliamna River a few years back, but I had little knowledge of the area. The conversation led to the great hunting and fishing in that area and the fact that he knew where there were 40 acres, with a lot of water frontage on Lake Iliamna, that he could purchase. The land was near Pedro Bay, a small Athabaskan village, and was part of Lillian Lapp's homestead that she obtained through the Alaska Native Land Claim settlement. Slim said that she would not sell me the land, but because he was a longtime friend of hers, he was sure she would sell it to him. The upshot of our conversation ended with Slim offering that we could become partners. I had to put up $60,000 to purchase the property, have it platted into lake front lots, with each of us keeping a lot, and Slim would sell the rest. We would make a sizable profit. Wow! Wow! My dream had come true. And besides … a pot of money waiting for me at the end of the rainbow. I could hear Judy Garland singing; "Somewhere … over the rainbow … skies are blue … and the dreams, that you dare to dream, really do come true …"

Alaska's Serengeti, Lake Iliamna, near Pedro Bay.
Photo by Verna Kolyaha of Pedro Bay, Alaska.

I'd like to tell you it all came true, but, to quote Robert Burns again, "The best laid schemes o' mice an' Men Gang aft a-gley." The story is too long and involved to tell, but after a couple years of pain, tears, attorneys, and money—I finally was the sole owner of the property. Slim and I have remained friends over the many years since the property was purchased.

In August of 1995, I had all the cabin materials flown to Pedro Bay. George Jacko Sr. (who would become a close friend) and his crew, loaded it all into several boats and motored it four miles down the lake, and unloaded it at the cabin site. A friend and builder, Dave Stewart, along with his son Mark helped me build a 10 x12 foot cabin in seven days. We selected a spot near a small protected bay, with a beautiful view south across the lake to the distant mountains. During the next few years, I flew out to Pedro Bay and worked on finishing the cabin: electrical, plumbing, insulation, and stained glass panels in the "biffy" that Sali designed. Over the last 28 years, family and friends have enjoyed times of fishing and recreation at the cabin. The only drawback is that the roundtrip airfare has gone from $90 in 1995 to $572 today. YIKES.

I named the bay, "Murphy's Bay," after my beloved Scottie who enjoyed going there with me. This remote area is really the "Serengeti" of Alaska, when you consider its vastness and minimal inroads by man—the beauty of the mountains, Lake Iliamna, (some 80 miles long and all drinkable), many crystal—clear rivers, Brown bears, caribou, moose, beavers, fresh water seals, all sorts of birds, and the largest sockeye salmon run in the world. It's a wilderness wonderland. God's country indeed.

George Jacko Jr., Pedro Bay Taxi.

Transportation to Pedro Bay.

Cabin view south.

Cam, pulling in a sockeye at Squirrel Point.

Tub of sockeyes.

Fillet time! Grandson, Justin, and Grandpa.

A nice sockeye.

Murphy's Bay Cabin.

Sali designed this stained glass window for the cabin biffy.

With friend and guide, George Jako Sr.

GONE AWRY

I'm a guy who doesn't mind being alone, so I frequently went out to my cabin with just my Scottie, Murphy, or "Mr. Woodro," as I sometimes called him. My family tolerated this unwise habit; however, it got me into trouble a few times. Fortunately, I managed to bail myself out without too much damage.

Slim owns 120 acres at the end of Long Bay that is not far from my cabin. This was the remainder of Lillian Lapp's homestead. She and her husband had built a nice two-bedroom cabin there. Slim used it as sleeping quarters for his bear hunting clients. Dave Stewart, his son Mark, and I used his cabin while building mine. During our time there, I noticed that on rainy days, the wind would drive water into the cabin at floor level.

One beautiful afternoon, I decided to go over to Slim's cabin to clean things up a bit and caulk the seam where the water came in. I took along my caulking gun and several tubes of caulk to solve the problem. When I reached the cabin, I noticed that a huge camouflaged parachute was spread out on the back lawn. It was the type used by the Army to drop a jeep or a 150 mm howitzer into a combat zone. I have no idea where Slim got it, but he had stored it in one of the tool sheds. The local Brown bears couldn't resist this plaything, and apparently enjoyed dragging it out into the yard. It had rained recently, and was so heavy. I couldn't lift or drag it, so I rolled it up into a huge ball and pushed it into a nearby wood shed. Another curious thing I noticed was a large number of old sparkplugs scattered around the front of the shed. I told this to Slim some months later, and he, being quite familiar with bear habits, said that bears like to play with such small objects. They like tossing them back and forth as kids do with a "Slinky."

After sweeping out the cabin and doing a few dishes, I began to caulk the outside of the floor seam to stop the water leak. I was just hummin' and happy, doing my neighborly good deeds. All was well. After going all around the cabin, I got to the last three feet along the front deck and needed to be on the ground to finish the caulking. The deck was only four or five feet above the ground—so, from a sitting position, with my legs over the edge of the deck, I gave a little push to drop to the ground.

Unbeknownst to me, there was a huge spike head sticking out of the edge of the deck, and it caught the leg of my jeans, right where the side and pocket seams come together. There I hung … two feet off the ground. I had no ability to grab anything. I reached around to the left and then to the right, trying to grab the edge of the deck, but no luck. There was nothing I could grab.

No one lived closer than a mile away, so yelling wouldn't help. There was no reason for anyone to come out to Slim's cabin, so that hope was gone. My flight back to Anchorage wasn't for 10 more days, so there was no reason to look for me. I wondered how long I could survive without water. Also if a Brown bear showed up ... I was a goner.

I had a vision of someone eventually finding my skeleton still hanging in my jeans next spring. With that picture in my mind, I knew I had to find a way to get myself out of this predicament!

Waving my arms around did nothing. I needed to move in a way that caused the pants to rip away from the spike head. The only thing I could do was to pull my knees up as far as possible, then quickly extend them, hoping the seam would split. I repeated this exercise over and over, and over again, until at long last ... my pants ripped, and I fell to the ground. Happily, I gathered my things together and headed back to my cabin. No meal for Mr. Brown bear today.

SQUIRREL POINT BEAR

One cloudless, warm July day, I motored a long way to Squirrel Point to catch a few sockeyes. Squirrel Point was even more remote than my cabin. No one lives within 10 miles. It's serious bear country, and there are always plenty of bear sign and salmon carcasses strewn along the beach. We've caught many sockeyes there, but it is a long way to go—about a 25-minute run by boat, with little protection from the prevailing east winds.

Lake Iliamna is one of only two lakes in the world that has fresh water seals. The other one is Lake Baikal in Russia. There is a small rocky island about 150 yards west of the Squirrel Point beach where the seals like to haul out to bask in the sun. On occasion, I can hear them barking at one another as I fish.

If the sockeyes are schooled up at the mouth of the small stream that flows into the lake, I pull my boat up into the stream, take out my fishing gear and cooler, and fish from shore. On this trip, the sockeyes were thick at the mouth of the stream. I'd usually catch five, clean and fillet them, place the fillets in the cooler, and then catch another four or five ... which is enough fishing and work for the day. My attention was primarily on fishing, but I did check up and down the beach every once in a while ... just in case Mr. Bear decided to come for a visit. After all, this was his territory, and I am the intruder who was stealing his dinner. The weather was good, the fishing was good, and my supply of trail mix was adequate—a perfect day.

For some reason, I felt a nudge to take a look up and down the beach. Usually, it was empty—except for the many flapping and squawking gulls that were waiting to eat the salmon carcasses I left behind. However, not this time. As I looked; out of the tall grass along the beach, about 150 yards away, stepped Mr. Brown bear. He casually strolled down to the water's edge, then turned to walk right toward me. His face and feet were black, but the rest of his body was light brown, almost blonde, and he was very bowlegged. My adrenalin level immediately went off the charts. I remembered reading that in such an instance one should make himself look big and make a lot of noise. I did this, but Mr. Bear just kept casually walking toward me. I did not want to shoot this bear. I already had a Brown bear hide hanging on a wall at home.

The boat was about 10 yards upstream from where I was fishing. I covered that distance in about two seconds and quickly checked my rifle. Then I threw all my gear into the boat, and pushed my loaded craft down the stream into the lake. I jumped in, and paddled like an Olympian to get far enough off shore in case I needed to start my trusty Evinrude. By now the bear was closing in on 40 yards away. I kept yelling and banging my paddle on the side of the boat. This didn't impress or scare the bear one bit. I finally sat down, and Mr. Bowlegged Bear just stared at me for a minute or two, then turned, and disappeared into the tall grasses once again. That was enough excitement for the day, so I cranked up my motor and headed back to Murphy's Bay… happy to have had a good day fishing and thanking God to be alive.

SMOKEY GOES FOR A SWIM

My trips to Murphy's Bay were usually in July and August. However, I remember one early October visit. I landed at the Pedro Bay airport to be met by my friend George Jacko Sr. I could sense that he was in a rush. George related to me that it was bear season and he was guiding for one of Slim's clients. These hunters had paid a $12,000 fee to get a shot at a trophy Brown bear.

There were so many bears in this area of Alaska that taking a nice bear was practically guaranteed. The frustrating problem that season, for both hunter and guide, was that no bears had been seen. This of course, put a lot of pressure on George and the other guides to get their hunter in position for a good shot. At a fee of $12,000 you don't want to send a hunter home without, at the very least, a decent shot at a Brown bear.

So, George passed me over to his youngest son Mike, to take me down to my cabin. Upon my arrival, I did my usual routine of uncovering the windows and checking out the place for bear damage. It is not unusual for bears to chew on the corners of the camp buildings and the deck edges. I have had to put four-foot pieces of aluminum angle on all the corners to slow the damage down. Unfortunately the bears seem to enjoy tearing the cedar siding off my cabin. That I can't protect, so we just patch it up and repaint the damage.

Fortunately, this time I saw no need for repairs. The next morning, the weather was a perfect October day—not a cloud in the sky, no wind, and temperatures in the 50s. A good day for the Michigan Wolverines to trounce the Ohio State Buckeyes. I made a pot of coffee and took a comfortable seat out on my deck. There, in the morning sun, I could view Murphy's Bay, the distant islands, and the far-off mountains to the south. Ah, life was good … French press coffee, beautiful weather, and awesome wilderness scenery. I had my chair tilted back against the cabin just soaking it all in. My distant gaze caught, what I thought, was one of my resident beavers as he swam into view around the point of a small island. This was a common sight, as there was a large beaver house at the end of a small cove about 50 yards past my cabin. I grabbed my binoculars to get a closer look. To my surprise, I wasn't looking at a beaver, but at the large head of a Brown bear. My first impulse was to retrieve my 7mm rifle from the cabin and get prepared for an easy shot. On further consideration, however, I didn't think I could haul this large dead bear up on shore to skin and then dispose of the carcass. Also, I didn't want to pay several hundred dollars to a taxidermist. So, I just watched as Smokey Bear silently swam by me and on into the cove opposite the beaver house. He never saw nor got scent of me. At the end of the cove, he climbed up the bank and shook the water off, looked around, and disappeared into the woods.

I pondered that just a few miles away was George and his bear hunting client, struggling and sweating to find a bear to shoot. As for me, a guy just having a cup of coffee on his deck, enjoying the beautiful scenery … and a trophy bear just casually swam right by me. "Mornin', Doc, how's things going?" "Doing well, doing well, Smokey, hope you are enjoying your morning swim." There's always something unusual and exciting going on in Murphy's Bay.

Mama bear showing off her cubs.

Smokey: 'See ya later, Doc!'

Bear damage.

TRAIL'S END

That's the end of a long trail I have led you down in this book. My personal life's trail is also nearing it's end. Certainly, I must be in the last chapter. My present age of almost 92, is pressing me to finish this book, started 18 + years ago on a rainy day in Girdwood. Oh, yes there are other stories and tales to tell, but they will have to wait till we are having lunch on a beautiful heavenly cloud.

Allow me to give you a Spiritual nudge. Life is all about' choices. Everyone makes choices, and choices have consequences. At the end of each day... we take our tired body, our soul, and our spirit to bed. On a good day, when we've made good choices, we have a clear conscience and are rewarded with a sound sleep. Mind and body are restored. We learn to heed the conscience God has given us to know right from wrong ... as well as to obey God's Word, the Bible, in making our life's decisions.

It all boils down to making every effort to choose to do the "right thing." I do not speak of perfection. We know from Scripture, "All sin and fall short of the glory of God" (Romans 3:23). Only Jesus lived a perfect life—a life without sin. It is because of Jesus's sacrificial death on the cross that Christian believers can be forgiven of their sins when confessed and followed by repentance.

In our lives, we will have trials, tribulations, and temptations. Our role in these times is to remain steadfast in trusting God to help us through to victory. Scripture tells us that life's hardships build endurance and character in us "We also glory in tribulations, knowing that tribulation produces perseverance; and perseverance, character; and character, hope. Now hope does not disappoint, because the love of God has been poured into our hearts by the Holy Spirit who was given to us" (Romans 5:3-5).

In every situation it's important to have a "right heart attitude," to enable us to do the right thing. This includes being a responsible person and putting into practice the fourth Commandment, "Honor your father and mother, that you may live long in the land that God gives to you."

Heartfelt forgiveness is a must. As we forgive others, God will forgive us. The Lord's Prayer clearly says "Forgive us our trespasses as we forgive those who trespass against us" (Matthew 6:12) as written in the Anglican Book of Common Prayer.

Determine to be a kind, courteous, thankful, forgiving, and loving person. There is an old saying, "Out of the soil of our lives some good should come" (Anon).

My hope and prayers are that you will have a blessed life, and a long life. That you will put God first in your life for as long as the Bell of Time rings for you. And that God will enable you to live your life with enthusiasm, and gratitude. That you will find joy in living with a loving, Christian mate and that God will bless you as He has blessed me.

Love,

Grampa, Great Grampa

ACKNOWLEDGEMENTS

I wish to thank my dear wife, Sali, for the many months she spent editing my book and helping me with the phrasing. I love the colorful cover she painted for the book.

I wish to thank my sister-in-law, Judy Stielstra, who graciously spent many hours editing my book and offering helpful suggestions as well. Also I would like to thank my brother-in-law, Elden Stielstra, for giving me the title of the book, *Day by Day.* Our daughter, Heather, deserves a special thanks for reading the entire book to help double check our corrections.

Also I wish to thank my editor, Marla McKenna, for her professional edit. The book benefitted greatly from her knowledge and skills. Amazingly, Marla and my best friend, Jack Rudell, who I wrote about in this book, have the same home town of Wausau, Wisconsin.

I would be remiss if I did not thank Carolyn Warren for giving her time and talent on a moment's notice to critique my book. Her comments were a great help to me in making *Day by Day* a more readable book. "Thank you so very much Carolyn."

I am thankful for the necessary help of my publisher, Mike Nicloy, who was found in an unusual way. A friend, Todd Findlay, who knew I was looking for a publisher, referred me to Kathy Tsiampas. Upon hearing the details of my book, she referred me to Luanne Nelson, both of whom had written two books. Luanne was excited to help me. She said, "I have the perfect publisher for you." So that's how I found Mike Nicloy. Obviously a higher power was at work in finding Mike.

Lastly, I am very thankful for all the encouragement and photographs given to me for the book by my family and friends. "Thank you all."

My hobby, carving decoys.

OUR FAMILY

Richard & Sali, with our great-granddaughter, Grace.

Our great-grandson, Jack Day Janowski, Jordan and Tyler's son

Our great-granddaughter, Evelene, Cam and Brittey's daughter.

Our daughter, Heather, and her husband, Paul.

Our granddaughter, Brittney, and our grandson-in-law-to-be, Cam, and our great-grandson, Curtis.

Our granddaughter, Natalie, her husband, Josh, and our great-grandson, Luke.

Our daughter, Holly, and her husband, Jon.

Our granddaughter Linnea's husband, Ryan, and our great-granddaughters, Keely and Keagan.

Our grandson, Richard, and our great-granddaughters, Sophia and Cambria.

Our grandson, Justin, his wife, Kara, our great-granddaughter, Grace, and great-grandson, Gavin.

Our grandson, Jordan, his wife, Tyler, our great-granddaughter, Penny, and great-grandson, Benjamin.

www.ingramcontent.com/pod-product-compliance
Lightning Source LLC
Chambersburg PA
CBHW051141120626
46547CB00012B/894